TORNADO
WARNING

A MEMOIR OF
TEEN DATING VIOLENCE
AND ITS EFFECT ON A WOMAN'S LIFE

TORNADO WARNING

A MEMOIR OF
TEEN DATING VIOLENCE
AND ITS EFFECT ON A WOMAN'S LIFE

Elin Stebbins Waldal

SOUND BEACH
PUBLISHING

Encinitas, California

Publisher's Cataloging in Publication Data

Waldal, Elin Stebbins.
Tornado warning : a memoir of teen dating violence and its effect on a woman's life /
Elin Stebbins Waldal. —Encinitas, Calif. : Sound Beach Pub., c2011.
p. ; cm.
ISBN: 978-0-9829813-0-6 (pbk.); 978-0-9829813-1-3 (ebook)
1. Dating violence. 2. Dating violence—Prevention. 3. Teenage girls—Abuse of.
4. Victims of dating violence—Psychological aspects.
5. Abused women—Psychological aspects. 6. Abusive men—Psychological aspects. I. Title.
HQ801.83 .W35 2011 2010913535
362.88/083—dc22 1102

Published by
Sound Beach Publishing
PO Box 235305, Encinitas, CA 92023
www.elinstebbinswaldal.com
www.tornadowarningbook.com
info@elinstebbinswaldal.com

Publishing Consulting and Product Development: BookStudio, LLC, www.bookstudiobooks.com
Editor: Terry Spohn
Copyediting: Laurie Gibson
Proofreading: Andrea Glass, The Writers Way
Book Design: Claudine Mansour Design, www.claudinemansour.com
Author photograph: Luke Pilon

Printed in the United States of America

Tornado Warning is a reflection of my life while living with an abusive boyfriend in my late teens. The journal entries in my memoir were originally written in 1986 while I was enrolled in the adult degree program at Vermont College of Norwich University. Working on that independent study, I referred to pieces I wrote while entrenched in that relationship, my sketch book/writing book, and my memory. The expository writing that accompanies the journal was written in the past two years. In some cases I referenced letters I had written or received to recall facts and emotions from my past.

This story is my truth, my experience, my memory; I am bringing this story out from the box in which it was stored to help others. Because these events happened many years ago, I have changed the names of people with whom I am no longer in contact or those who requested not to be named for their own personal reasons. Although I did not change the geography, I did change the names of houses, restaurants, and bars that I frequented during that time.

*This book is dedicated to the countless individuals who
have suffered at the hands of a loved one;
may you find peace and healing in your journey and know
that your life has meaning and purpose.
Every human being and living creature deserves
a life free from torment of any kind;
there is no excuse for abuse.*

FOREWORD

THERE ARE A few moments in your life when you know someone special has walked into it. And that's exactly how I felt when I met Elin Stebbins Waldal. We are two women divided by a stretch of California coast and a variety of different life experiences; while Elin's area of expertise is teens and dating, mine is confidence and self-esteem. We are two women united in our mission to help every single young woman out there recognize her self-worth and to engage in her life as a full, vital force. We both recognize the vulnerability of teens. We both see that many teens are more worried about what others think of them than what they think of themselves. And we have both experienced the sometimes devastating results of an outer-directed or compromised self-image.

I actually met Chandler, Elin's daughter, before I met Elin. She was a bright star amongst the teenage crowd of participants at a speaking event I was keynoting. Chandler and I connected immediately; her wit and wisdom told me one thing: she must have come from good parents! Chandler was eager to speak up, share her vision, and help other girls see their powerful potential. I wish that many of the teens I meet and work with could have the confidence that Chandler possesses. But all too often our teen girls have their sense of self subtly, imperceptibly whittled away by others—whether friends, parents, or a boyfriend or girlfriend—so that what is left of that courageous, energetic teen is a shell tumbled by the tides, a flowerless stem bending to the prevailing winds.

As soon as I heard about Elin's book, I got goose bumps. That is my (non-scientific) sign for knowing that I have stumbled onto a synergistic message. I immediately responded to the stupendous courage it takes to share her devastating story of her teenage-self and how she came to be over-powered and controlled by a young man who claimed to love her. Elin is willing to reveal her own painful history to help you understand the short- and long-range effects of an abusive relationship. She is willing to tell her story to protect teens, like her daughter Chandler and her son's Kodiak and Max, and she is asking you to recognize that teens everywhere, from small towns and big cities, rich families and poor, are all very vulnerable at this time in their lives.

When you read this book I have no doubt you will find shreds of your own teenage insecurity in it. Elin does a beautiful job making her story your own. This book is as much a cautionary tale as it is a brilliant celebration of Elin's ability to now get out there and inspire young people to help find and hold onto their authentic selves. A true testament to triumph over tragedy, Elin has created a new career path as a speaker to teach students about healthy and unhealthy relationships. And she is the fearless founder of Girls kNOw More, an organization dedicated to creating intimate parent/daughter groups that encourage conversations on today's hot button teen topics.

To say that I admire the courage Elin exhibits in unlocking the pages of her journal and sharing them openly with the world would be an understatement. She has taken a tattered part of her personal story and sewn it back together with such unflinching and loving honesty that it will no doubt awaken all parents out there to the insidious nature of abuse in teen relationships.

Her story serves as a warning to parents. This book is for our daughters and our sons. Do not be complacent. Abuse does not discriminate so pay attention to the signs and keep open the channels of communication with your children. Their lives could depend on it.

—JESS WEINER,
self-esteem expert and author of
Life Doesn't Begin 5 Pounds from Now and *A Very Hungry Girl*
www.jessweiner.com

UNGUARDED

In the palms of my hands
the beauty of living rests
deeply I feel, deeply I fall
hands open, hands extended
rising in the depth of my soul
but for a whisper of weight . . .
is the sensation of love.

—ELIN STEBBINS WALDAL

INTRODUCTION

"Courage is the most important of all the virtues,
because without courage you can't practice any other virtue consistently.
You can practice any virtue erratically,
but nothing consistently without courage."

—MAYA ANGELOU

DAY TWENTY-ONE POST-hysterectomy: doctor's orders have me bound to a couch with books. I have just finished reading an entire young adult series that girls and women alike are enthralled with. Now in the light of the morning I sit drumming the closed cover of the last book. I am thinking of my teenage years to the point where they play in front of me like a film. I am fighting for my life, half in the shadow and half in the light. I see myself so clearly. I want to stop him, help her—help the young woman who was me that flickers before my eyes. The daylight streaming in from the window is so bright it's blinding. Under most circumstances I would close the curtain in annoyance. But not now. My anger solves nothing, so I pull it back and let the light of truth pour in. I am at the high end of my forties and I finally can say out loud, "I am one of the one in three women who have been abused."

The book rests on my lap just below the wound where my uterus and cervix made their unceremonious exit from my body. I think about the three lives I have birthed. I should be dead, I think—but I am not. Why have I not told my story? There was a false start in my early twenties when I gave voice to my teenage self by writing about it. After, I gathered up the pages of my story and, much like tying a gag around my own mouth, placed the pages into a shoe box. What has hiding my unfinished story in a box done for my children? Romances will be written and read, love will be glamorized until the end of time—people crave an escape and I don't blame them. There is something so compelling about made-up love, page-turning drama where the hero saves the day and no matter how scary things get, everything works out and the couple rides happily off into the sunset. But that is not my story.

Jimmy walks into the room and my fingers come to a rest on the book cover. I stare at him, and in that split second he sees it so clearly etched on my face that he sits down. "You've decided, huh?" And that's when I know the decision I have made is cemented. "Yup, the time is now." He nods and reaches over and puts his hand on top of mine. "Good, I think that is good, seriously . . . I think you should." Of course he has listened to me grumbling my way through the roughly 2,500 pages of fiction. He also listened to me tell him about my friends' responses when I mentioned I was thinking about going back to work on my book—a wake-up call that sounded like this: "I've heard it before, Elin. Stop talking about it and do it."

At first only Jimmy, our oldest son Max, and a handful of family and friends knew I was writing full time. I didn't know where my journey would lead, so, much like a pregnancy, I kept it to myself for the first few months. But pages were printed, and I was often discovered by our younger two at the kitchen table banging away at the keys of my laptop. I wanted my kids to know, but I didn't want to be premature about telling them. I was sorting, sifting, trying to make my way without explaining.

Their curiosity was inevitable. One night Kodiak and Chandler, jackets on, ready to go to a movie, waiting for Jimmy to get off the phone with a client, cornered me in the kitchen. *They* had questions—what could I possibly be writing about? How could *anyone* have that much to say about *anything*?

The kids continued to pepper me with questions—and I moved things around, trying to stall before answering them.

"Well, what *are* you writing about?"

I knew there was no escape; Jimmy was still yammering away and I had to come clean. "Since you've asked, I have gone back to writing a book that I began over twenty years ago."

"A *book*?" in unison. "What's it about?"

I felt the mask of doubt cover my face. How much should I say?

"Come on, Mom . . . "

"OK, I'll tell you the story, but I need to preface this by saying I am not going to tell the entire story." I began to unfold what for so many years I had considered to be my dirty laundry. Now telling these truths, hanging them on an imaginary line before my children, I could almost feel the fresh air and sunshine the airing out would provide.

To allow them to see what woke me up to my reality, I brought them to one of the more horrific nights with Derrick. In detail I told them. For a moment it was very still.

Kodiak's eyes were on me. Was he breathing? "Mom, I can't believe that happened to you . . . I can't imagine anyone wanting to hurt you."

"All's I know is if someone tried any of that on *me*, I would kick their butt and then leave. No way—not even one second chance. *No!*" My daughter's response reminded me of something I myself might have said at her age.

"Kodiak, promise me you will never ever hurt some girl like that!" she barked.

"Chandler, I would never . . . "

It is hard to explain to anyone, much less your children, how it happens. The incipience of abuse is not fully detectable; hooks are planted so deeply in your skin that your body adjusts to the feel of them. Derrick made me believe I was his anchor to the world, that somehow if I were to vanish, so would he.

My kids in the end galvanized me. I want a better world for all three of them, their cousins, friends, and really, all people. No one should have to live in fear.

Knowing that acceptance is paramount to freedom, I will no longer remain silent. I was once battered, a victim trapped in the clench of what is known as the cycle of violence. My liberation has been engendered by my ability to accept that my past does not define me. I am a survivor, therefore I am no longer a victim. I am a woman, therefore I do not choose to always identify myself as a survivor. Like all women I am a kaleidoscope of my myriad roles and experiences; there is not one label that sums me up.

It would not occur to me to characterize myself as an extraordinary person. I have no one gift that would make someone clamor to be in my company. I have led an ordinary life, enjoyed a happy childhood, with loving parents at the helm, surrounded by three brothers and a sister, all of whom made me feel I was special.

In the cradle of this life I led as a child I was confident. I vividly recall at the age of five pinching myself and saying, "I AM ME." Three raw words of a near-baby would shape my life in a way I could not have understood at the time.

I grew up mostly in Old Greenwich, Connecticut, a bedroom community of New York City. There was a move to Houston for five-and-a-half years—years that formulated my voice inflections and left remnants of a drawl when we moved back to the hometown of my infancy the year I turned ten.

I am the daughter of a minerals geologist and an editor-turned-entrepreneur. People greeted my parents formally throughout the village. "Good morning, Mr. Stebbins, how are you on this fine Saturday? Ah, is that your little girl?" A chuckle bubbles up in Dad's throat and he shakes his head. I know it's because he doesn't think of me as "his" nor does he think of me as "little." The merchant, confused, takes the dress shirts from my father and states, "Soft and folded," even though he knows the answer. "Yes, thank you, Frank." As we depart I hear Frank call his parting salutation, "Have a great day, Mr. Stebbins."

My mother couldn't get more than a few steps into the Foodmart without seeing a friend and, of course, in those days void of cellular connection, people stopped to talk. This provided me the pleasure of finding grocery items to place covertly into the basket without the well-trained eyes of my mother upon me. Checking out at the OG landmark of a grocery store, all the employees also knew the Stebbins family elders by name. "Hi, Mrs. Stebbins, how are you today? Would you like carry-out service?" The cordial niceties that existed in the small-town life that was prevalent in the 1970s of course made us all feel safe.

It was a picturesque childhood. This was a community where my dad biked to the train station and we children walked to school. Where stores closed on Sunday, and the local stationery shop later provided my first punch-clock job. We had a beach open to residents only, Tod's Point, and we all had cards that proved we belonged. In the summer months we biked there and played in the Long Island Sound until our skin was golden and freckled and our hair bleached with sun and breeze. People didn't loiter, and homelessness was something that existed in the bowels of New York City.

It was a New England community founded in the year 1640, steeped in a tradition of higher education, civility, and adults who spawned children filled with promise. Not exactly a town where subjects like "domestic and teen dating violence" were topics at cocktail parties. The ugly secret lay tucked into bedrooms, living rooms, and dens. Walls that bore witness to brutality, anguish, and desperation—that at times shouldered the blow of a shoved body, a human spirit crumpled beneath the damaged sheetrock, wondering if this was the time it would be extinguished.

If you were to wend your way through any neighborhood when the light of day fades to dark, with all the lights aglow, you might catch a glimpse into a housed life. A life that at first blush may appear to conform to the fairy-tale living that was portrayed in television of long ago. Look again. In the glow of electric light, there are as many unhappy stories unfolding as there are happy. For some, discord is as normal as the sun coming up at the break of day. They are trapped in a vicious cycle of torment and fear, and the very concept of safety is foreign. Yes, even in Old Greenwich, Connecticut, people fall victim to violence at the hands of someone who loves them. Women, men, children, doctors, lawyers, custodians, delivery drivers, teachers, bank presidents, educated, uneducated. No one dreams it will happen to them. God knows I didn't.

TORNADO
WARNING

A MEMOIR OF
TEEN DATING VIOLENCE
AND ITS EFFECT ON A WOMAN'S LIFE

THIS MORNING I am the first awake and my reward is the near stillness. I am alone with my thoughts; I know few women who wouldn't bask in quiet the way one would a sunny spot on a cool day.

My reservoir of quiet is usurped as the day unwraps itself to my daily life. It is one filled with the routine that children bring—breakfast conversation, lunch-packing, teeth-brushing, jacket-grabbing, backpack-shouldering, kiss-giving mornings. Only this morning when the quiet returns it is competing with the rumbling buzz of my mind absorbed in the vision of Chandler disappearing around the corner on her bicycle headed to school. Her freedom and innocence are caught tight as a lump in my throat. That image of her bike turning the corner brings to mind the many corners she will round, a future that is yet untold. Will I see her as she barrels forward in time?

While Chandler swam inside my body, what I imagined was the grown woman who would years later become my friend. My imagination soared through the sky like an arrow past the changing of diapers, redirecting of behavior, homework, the at-times unpopular role of constant mentor, and landed squarely on the bull's-eye of her adulthood.

Thinking about that fantasy, it all makes sense—my relationship with each of my parents blossomed in adulthood once I had eclipsed the period of my life where I needed them. Watching her ride away I am acutely aware of how much she will need me for many more years to simply be her mother.

During my sophomore year my parents moved from Old Greenwich to Stamford, into a beautiful old farmhouse that belonged to a longtime family friend. The property was gorgeous, with large trees that begged to be climbed and the remnants of a barn that burned long before we pulled in the drive. In the back just off the formal living room was a screened-in porch that was reminiscent of the waterfront home that now stood firmly planted in my rearview mirror along with the houses we had moved from. In many ways I loved this house but more for the privacy its enormous yard afforded. What I did not love was that it was located beyond the school district boundary of Greenwich High School, where all my friends were. Initially my parents did not see the school down the road as an option; we looked at several alternatives and in the middle of tenth grade I went to boarding school. I went, but I did not stay. Three weeks in I threatened to leave. "Canada or home," I remember telling my mother defiantly, and days later I was home.

Many years after, mom told me that while dropping me off at school I waved her off with a kiss and a hug as if we had been accustomed to a life apart. The thought of her walking out of that building with not as much as a backward glance from me makes me ache for her. That moment must have been brutal. She reached her car, cried—and began the process of letting me, the last of her children, go.

What that must have been like—excruciating comes to mind. I was only fifteen. Is it more difficult with the last? Do we really ever let go?

I finished the school year at the local school, living at home. During that time I hatched a plan for my return to Greenwich High School, and that was how I ended up living with my girlfriend Alex and her family.

Living at Alex's house was akin to living on my own minus the re-sponsibility of bill paying. I had no hard-and-fast rules that bound me to a schedule and I was accountable primarily to myself. A basement bed-room with its own entrance meant I could come and go as I wished an independence that served to fuel my desire for emancipation. At the close of my junior year my parents moved back within the school boundaries, I moved home again, which was like putting on a shoe that didn't fit.

The start of my senior year of high school on many levels was spring fed by a combination of events that made for the perfect storm. The freedoms I experienced at Alex's house vanished as soon as I crossed the threshold of my parent's new home. I was brokenhearted because Fergus, my boyfriend of the past year, had left for college and subsequently ended our relationship. Many of my friends had graduated, which left a void for those of us remaining. The emptiness I felt was constant, a thirst that nothing seemed to quell.

I was on a one-way street heading into oncoming traffic, blind to the danger around the bend. At seventeen I met a guy who was older, living on his own, and running his own business. It was the equivalent to winning the dating jackpot. That exhilaration was underscored by the fact that he found me attractive, mature, and put-together.

Hi E-Babes!

Wow, what a weekend and am I ever psyched, Yes!!! Man, he's as cool as I have been imagining all along. I am so happy! I figure I better get this all down on paper as proof that things besides school are going partly my way! I swear I figured my whole social ability was shot since Fergus left for college, but hey it appears the kid still has some appeal after all.

All the BS that's been going on with Mark and Becka? Yeah, well she finally told him, "Seeyamuchlater" . . . better yet . . . "asinnever"!

Man, what a baby he is. I cannot begin to imagine how Becka put up with him for as long as she did. I guess the night he hauled off and backhanded her woke her up. Personally? I think the guy is a psycho.

Anyway, because of all this stuff with Mark, Becka didn't go over to the party at Meadow Wood this past weekend . . . but I did . . . so there I am partying with everyone then along comes Mark (Puhleaze, like I want to talk to him after what he did to Becka!) but of course he wants to talk to me 'cause I am like Lucy in the Peanuts comic strip with her flippin' sign up except without "5¢" on it. No . . . I have the invisible sign on my forehead; it reads "Will listen for free." Ugh!!!!

So of course there's a break in conversation and Mark says, "Hey . . . um Elin . . . um can I talk to you?"

"I don't know, dipstick, can you?" is what I am thinking but of course don't say.

"Sure." So I follow him toward the entrance to his room but stop outside the door as if to say, "Right here, no further." He rolls his eyes but doesn't push it. "OK, Mark, ya got me over here—what?" So I am looking into his face and it actually goes through my mind that he looks a little hammered.

"Jeez, a little hostile? What? What did I do?"

"Mark, look, you asked for the conference call, you got it. What?"

So he just starts in . . . what an idiot Becka is, how he treated her like a queen and how she can just break up with him like that is beyond him. Blah, blah, blah, blah . . . Inside I am just getting more and more pissed off. Becka is my friend. What the hell, who does he think he is to just throw all his screwed-up mistakes to the side and act as if he were exonerated of any wrong doing. Finally, I put my hand up. "Stop," it silently yells at him.

"Stop," I say, 'cause clearly by his rambling, he didn't catch it.

"What?!" his face all screwed up like a little kid who just got caught stealing candy from the store.

"What? You ask me what? You're kidding. Right? You really can't be that irretrievably stupid!" I actually felt sweat burst from my underarms. Shit, how far can I push him? But I am pissed, so I use the adrenaline. "You, Mark, you have yourself to blame. You frickin' blew it! You should have stopped to consider how great you had it; Becka is an awesome girl. You hit her. What'd ya think? Huh? That she was gonna just stick around for you to lose it again. You fucked up! You, Mark. Not Becka!"

Now the sweat bursts to my palms. His eyes are bulging. I actually wonder if he is going to pop a vein. And then I just had to add, "She'd be here tonight if you knew what you had before you frickin' stomped on her like a used-up, smoldering cigarette—she'd still be with you. Call yourself the idiot. Idiot. Not my friend!"

Uh, yeah, that pushed him over the edge. Anyone who knows Mark knows he can't handle the booze he drinks, much less the truth from a 5'5" girl.

He pushes me up against the wall (yeah, he's about 210 lbs and stands 6'2". There's a contest. I'm what, 112?) and spits his foul beer breath in my face and starts yelling at me. Not talking with his teeth clamped but yelling.

"It's you! You bitch—you told her to stay away from me! Not to come to the party tonight, not to answer my phone calls . . . what the hell, Elin? I can't believe you!"

To say I was just a little nervous would be like the quintessential under-statement of the century. Thank frickin' goodness Jillian walked into the room. Man, she took one look at me with Mark looming over me pinned to the wall and she freaked like only Jillian knows how to freak! So yeah, she just bolted into the living room and apparently she announced to the whole party that Mark was about to kill me. The next thing I know there's Derrick (followed by various and sundry other people) but I saw him and, trust me dear diary, he did not need a white horse or shining armor, the work boots and levis were just fine!

For a guy who's at least five inches shorter and God knows how much lighter than Mark, he sure did let him have it.

"What the hell are you doing, Mark? Get the fuck away from her, what is your problem? What the hell are you doing anyway? You think it's cool to intimidate her like that 'cause you're bigger? What, huh? You gonna hit her? What the hell is wrong with you? Get off her, man. I may not know much but I know this—you never, ever treat a girl like that."

Wellllll, after that, yes, thank you fans! Derrick took me to his room and we hung out the rest of the night, just talking about stuff. He is so cool. I plan to get to know him a lot better. I mean really . . . look how protective he was over me, he hardly knows me. I am thinking the attraction is mutual. I can't wait for tomorrow, I am so heading to Meadow Wood after school.

LIKE MANY TEENS, I was on a mission to step outside the boundary lines that my siblings blazed before me, and my rebellion involved among other things, alcohol. What began as a thrill later provided a numbing effect from the brutality I was suffering. I became adept at painting a portrait of a girl who had it together on the outside, yet on the inside the canvas was more like spin art.

It was called an Ass Kicker, according to teenage folklore. This is where the teen in the house raids the liquor cabinet and, because she is inexperienced, pours all available liquids into a plastic jar. Brown, clear, green, red . . . who knows . . . whatever wasn't stuck to the cabinet I stealthily lifted and carefully tilted to avoid causing any suspicion. After that I added whatever soda was available to mask the bitter flavor of the booze. In our house, that soda was Dr. Pepper. It was pretty gross.

"You are *so* lucky, because you get to do whatever you want and your parents never care!" my then-quite-innocent friend Jeanne proclaimed with envy. We were fourteen turning fifteen, and she reminds me to this day that I corrupted her. Jeanne, on the other hand, was under the watchful eye of her mother. I introduced Jeanne to everything from sailing to music, boys to drinking—in short, my versions of freedom.

I can honestly say that while I was growing up my parent's ritual of sitting down for an evening drink seemed completely and utterly normal; most of my friends' parents did the same. To this day I can hear my mother telling me that sitting down every evening to enjoy a cocktail was relaxing. I get that, it is—and that was one of the indelible impressions tattooed on my childhood.

Hi E,

Lately Kelli and I have gotten a lot closer, we have been hanging around doing stuff together. She's pretty cool. She told me she used to hate me. She said I was a snob. A snob? I still can't figure that out. I am way too shy to be a snob . . . or so I thought.

I am a self-conscious freak. If anything I feel as if people don't notice me, kind of like the blend-in type of person. I guess not so much with my close friends, they all know I am not shy or whatever but snob? Wow. I have nothing to be stuck up about . . . I am average to look at, I am neither popular nor unpopular, I can sing (that's something) but I don't think I have been snobbish about that. What else? Kelli is one of those really gregarious types. In some ways I envy her; she is quick on her feet and always busting on the guys. She knows stuff about cars and rides motorcycles. Puhleaze, what guy wouldn't like a girl who rides dirt bikes? Oh yeah and who is also pretty, has a great figure, and is funny! I think they call that the full package?

Anyway, she is fun and apparently she's gotten over my "snotty attitude," so that's cool. What else . . . So Kelli's brother Jack—oh my God, Jack? I remember him from last year when I lived at Alex's house—he was dating Alex's sister Isabel's friend Gabby and they came over a few times. Anyway, he's good friends with Derrick and his brother Brett. Yeah, well yesterday Kelli and I were leaving school and she asked if I wanted to go back to her house for a BBQ later on. Her parents were out of town so she told me Jack was having people over. Hmmmm. Uh yeah, how about not a minute to think about that. Duh! So after work I head over to her house and I just about have my heart in my throat 'cause Brett's truck (The Truck) is in the driveway and usually Derrick is with Brett. I of course have seen Derrick a couple of times this week at Meadow Wood and we talked and all but it's not like we were alone a lot or anything. Anyway, so Kelli and I head into the kitchen and all these people are there. I see Derrick and he comes over and gives me a hug (?). OK, wow. I thought I was going to pass out . . . and then he introduces me to a few people as his girlfriend. I look over at Kelli and she is just smiling away and I am thinking, did I miss something or what? Derrick pulls me aside and says to me, "That's OK, right? I mean I really like you and I for sure want to hang out a lot more and . . . " Yeah, he saw the hand but unlike Mark he didn't need the verbal queue on top of it.

"Yeah . . . it's OK, I feel the same . . . nervous, but yeah."

I am standing there thinking to myself, is this really happening? It's all so weird. I mean let's start with the truck.

OK diary, I know. What about the truck? I have noticed this old truck for probably about three years. It's an old Jeep and it has these wood sides that you can tell someone made and the truck is black and I constantly see

it around. I have always thought it was kind of . . . I don't know . . . cute?
Cute for a truck. Oh, that sounds so stupid but anyway (you don't care). So
the truck is Brett's truck—and now Derrick tells me he is buying it from Brett
'cause Brett wants a bigger truck.

Isn't that weird? It's not like I am saying there is some mystical thing
here, but it's sort of like the truck has been on the fringe of my life and I was
destined to collide with it.

Whatever.

So the rest of the party was surreal for me except for this weird thing with
Brett that shook me from my inebriation. Derrick and I were on the porch and
we hear all this commotion, mostly Jack laughing and saying, "That-a boy,
Rex, you tell him," but then we hear Brett's voice telling Jack he's gonna kick
his stupid dog's ass and Jack's too if he ever bites him again. Derrick and I
follow the noise. Jack is just laughing at Brett, saying something like, "Yeah,
ya gonna fuckin' beat me and my dawg," and he's totally mocking Brett—you
know, using a tough guy accent to sound . . . I don't know . . . like a NY Italian
or something. Kelli all of a sudden pipes in, "What'd ya think, you big jerk,
he was just gonna let you bite him and not retaliate? You got what you de-
serve." (See??? Love her!!!!) I am totally lost at this point and I say, "What?
You bit Jack?" Then Jack really starts laughing and he says, "No . . . he bit
Rex . . . my dog." I am standing there with my jaw on the floor and I say to
Derrick, "He bit the dog?" Derrick takes me by the hand and leads me back
to the porch and says, "Brett likes to hassle dogs . . . just stay away from him."

"Wait a minute . . . what do you mean he 'hassles' dogs?"

"My brother can be kind of an asshole. He picks on dogs and people and
pretty much whatever he feels like. Don't worry, he's cool, just kind of has
a short fuse."

"Short fuse? Um . . . that's screwed up, who picks on a dog . . . especially
all these sweet dogs."

"Hey, let's forget about it, huh?" and he kisses me. Derailed, not totally
expecting that.

Very sweet . . . not Fergus. (Yeah . . . did I say that?) No, it was good. I
mean, the rest of the night was great, we had fun and I am really excited
'cause I really do like Derrick. It's confusing. I still love Fergus but he's not
here and he made the rules "better to just be friends." OK, yeah, I get it but I

am not gonna just sit around and wait for him to come home. I gotta some-how move on, forget about that. Besides, Derrick sees me as his girlfriend!

The dog thing is bugging me. Ella, that's Brett's dog, is such a sweetie, but she always seems like she is cowering a little bit and so now after the biting deal I don't wonder. Then there's Abby, Derrick's dog, and of course there is Rex. It is so weird seeing Jack at his house. He always seemed so much older than Alex and me. All those guys are. Not sure if they finished high school or what. Derrick and Brett do odd jobs: firewood, masonry . . . stuff. Jack is pretty much a mason. Derrick is twenty-one; not sure about Brett, but he's older, so I don't know, twenty-three? Jack's probably Isabel's age and she's the same age as my brother John . . . who's three plus years older than me so . . . he's twenty-one-ish maybe? Whatever . . . who cares really? I wish every so often I were done with high school, I don't know, some-times I just long for it to be all behind me, over, in the rearview mirror, done.

SOME THINGS IN life I can set my clock by. The dog sighs expectantly waiting for our morning run. Moments later, our habits perfected, we are on the sidewalk. Chinook pulls me in anticipation while I admonish her for her enthusiasm, set my watch, adjust my iPod, and think about which way to go—all before we hit the curb. Once in the street, the road spills out before us and we are off. The thing about running is it clears my head. My feet pound the pavement; I see my bossy alpha dog in my periphery, her chocolate brown coat shimmering in the sun, and I am so glad for her place in my life.

Chinook and I choose the lagoon trail today, which wends its way alongside a saltwater shoal that stretches a mile wide until it narrows be-fore it pours into the Pacific. Along the trail a person can spy 185 species of birds, my favorite of which remains the hawk. The path is well traveled by explorers of all ages, many of whom have their canine buddies in tow. It is another sun-filled, cloudless day. The air is a bit chilly but not enough to warrant a jacket. I feel cheered by the sun and embrace my ability to move with vigor.

On the other side of the country on a much chillier day, my parents met on a ski slope in Stowe, Vermont. Their story was a touchstone of my childhood, the genesis of the Stebbins family. When I was growing up, this story was a textbook illustration for me of what falling in love should be like. I believed I, too, would just *know*, or there would be some sort of sign that would show me that he was the one. Mom glimpsed my father at the bottom of the mountain and that is where, she says, it was simple prophecy on her part. She saw it—the pipe, the slippers, the future—and he in his utter oblivion and youth had no idea what was set in motion. With purpose, she collided with him at the "top turn of the nosedive." After getting back to their feet they stood and admired one another's skis. Dad's tips were painted with words that would later be inscribed in both of their wedding rings, "Ho-La-Hi, Ho-La-Ho," and Mom had a sprig of holly painted on hers.

They parted for downward slopes. She knew he went to MIT and that his nickname was Stebby, and that much she shared with her mother upon her return home. Days later my grandmother found the results for MIT's ski team. He had placed. The future geologist and father of five, Robert H. Stebbins was auspiciously posted in the paper as a winner.

Dad would say that he was surprised by the gift he received from Elinor L. Fairchild of Pelham. He held the hat up and out dropped the note. "This is a magic hat. Wash only in melted snow."

That truck of Derrick's was my sign. I remember feeling that it somehow had been rolling around town trying to get me to see that the man of my dreams was in it. I was fixated on weaving a story for my own future children much in the way the stocking hat was passed on to me.

Hey E,

I am so in love with him!!! We have so much fun together it's like every day is a new adventure. We are always going somewhere . . . sometimes we four-wheel drive into the backwoods and then just hang and talk. Other days we just lie around in bed while everyone else is off doing whatever it is they are doing without us.

"What drew you to me?" I ask him with my head resting on his shoulder.

"Wow . . . where did that come from?"

I trace a smile on his chest and look up at his face. "Just curious . . . we kind of bumped into each other, but it was like a magnet or something. You kind of pulled me in. So I was curious, what drew you to me?"

His green eyes light up in amusement and he grabs my hand that is drawing and places it over his heart and I can feel its thrum under my fingertips.

"It was a lot of things . . . ," he whispers with a kiss to my hair.

I withdraw from him and sit up. "You are so not off the hook with that answer . . . come on, I want to know. Why me?"

I haphazardly tie my hair in a knot and wait for his answer.

"Well, for starters, there was the crazy Mark incident . . . it just set me over the edge seeing you like that . . . you seemed so . . . I don't know . . . little and helpless." His eyes are locked on mine now.

"Little and helpless?! What?!"

"Hey, you asked . . . " His voice trails off, a little defensive.

"No, I know . . . go on . . . but to be clear, I am so not little and helpless. Carry on."

"OK, Miss Not-Little-and-Helpless, as I was saying . . . I guess the other thing was just your ability to talk with me. I mean a lot of girls your age are so . . . clueless or something. But not you, you have it together and I love that. I mean, you're right, you're not 'helpless,' but I wanted to kick his butt

that night, I mean, we had just begun our flirtation and seeing him like that just made me see red." At this he looks down.

"See red? And that means . . . ?"

"You know, like an expression . . . It's when I can't think about anything but hurting someone."

"And this is a common sensation?" I ask, smiling.

Now he looks up at me again, also smiling. "No . . . no . . . nothing like that, just, I don't know, that night I wanted to hurt Mark for being such an idiot to you. I mean, who the hell did he think he was towering over you like that. It was bullshit. Anyway, all I know is I have fallen completely in love with you, I love your smile, your sarcasm toward my brother, your sense of humor . . . everything."

"You love me?"

"Yeah, what'd ya think? I was just messing with your head here?"

"No, no, of course not. I love you, too."

"Good, 'cause now that you're mine, I'm not letting you go."

So that was my day!! I'm back home now and I am just beaming! He is so sweet. I love that he is older, he is so much more mature than a lot of the guys I know. He had to grow up pretty fast. His parents were divorced when he was kind of young and neither one of them really seemed to want his brother or him, or that's the way he makes it sound. So they both got it together and made their own way, you know, working and stuff.

Anyway . . . enough about all that, we are talking about camping up at Pound Ridge with a group of people this weekend. That will be so much fun! I love it up there!

THE GIDDY THRILL of crisis and excitement, and the passion that the intensity of that group of guys infused was intoxicating. At home it was just Mom and me. Having been at Alex's for a year, I had grown accustomed to zipping in and out without notice, and I imagined my mother had adjusted to Dad working out of state and me living somewhere else. I took liberties to maintain my freedom, misled my mother about where I was going and what I was doing. She had no reason to believe I was leading a secret life. I wasn't in trouble. My grades were decent, I didn't skip classes, I had a job. I don't think it occurred to her to think anything but that I was doing what teenagers in high school did.

When Derrick entered my life, the feeling of rejection I experienced when Fergus departed was erased. In some ways I believe the appeal of Derrick rested solely in how different he was from Fergus. Derrick was the perfect diversion. He was older, came off as completely independent, owned a business, and had a tough exterior that was intriguing. I mistook that bravado and thought of him as experienced in a way that felt worldly to me.

And of course there was the truck I had seen around for all those years. My fantasy world was at play and it usurped any sensors that may have detected the cracks in Derrick's mask. There were always great parties happening, and when we were together it was exhilarating to be seen as this cool girl, his girlfriend. I was seventeen while most of his friends were well into their twenties, so it made me feel older, which is exactly what I was programmed to believe I was supposed to be. I can still hear my father's voice saying as if it were high praise, "Elin is five going on thirty."

When I was seven and we still lived in Houston, I recall standing in the large double-door entry to the living room in my long flannel nightgown, surveying the room. Dad was animated amid his guests, smoke swirling as if a light fog had arrived.

"There she is!!" He gestured me to come to him and on a cloud of anticipation, I went to his embrace. "How about a song, huh, big girl?"

Oh how we loved the spotlight. My dad was larger than life in that moment—beaming with pride over my willingness to perform. He loved music and all of his songs wrapped around us like his old army sleeping bag, providing a cocoon to climb back into if only in a hummed-out tune. From the ski songs to the old folk songs, the words are underscored by their melodies, refrains of which repeat over and over, in a way keeping him alive forever. "Down by the Station," "The Logger," "White Coral Bells." Dad's voice was capable of quieting a room full of kids spread out on a sleeping porch, drowning out fears of spiders and creaking noises with the refrain "Dona Nobis Pacem Pacem."

Give us peace.

In many respects Dad died on May 25, 2005, and not the February 10, 2006, date typed on his death record. That cerebrovascular accident robbed him of his speech, his mobility, his felicity, and his dignity. The death certificate in my hand summarizes the aggregate, data-driven facts of his life: eighty-one, male, white, social security number. I survey the document as if looking for some clarity or insight into Robert Harnden Stebbins. "Geologist" was his "Last Known Occupation" and "Exploration" was his "Stated Industry." Exploration. I can picture that because we have slides from his past, such as Dad alongside the bicycle that carried him all over Nova Scotia. My dad, the modern-day explorer.

I was in a training seminar when the text message scrolled across my cell phone: "Dad had a stroke. Not sure the extent of the damage. Call me." My brother didn't need to sign off; my phone told me who sent the message. I was in Newport Beach, California, and it was 10:30 a.m. PST. By 7:00 a.m. EST the next day I was in Paul's arms at the airport in Richmond, Virginia.

"Ah, E-Babes, weren't we just here?" he whispered. Fighting tears, I nodded, and we escaped the flurry of travelers. Paul's rented car was equipped with a mechanism called "Never Lost," a GPS system designed to get us to the hospital and the phantasmagorical world of ICU. I stared at the bold yellow letters, "Never Lost," and considered the possibility that we could navigate our way to a different time, a different place, a different reason for being. A stroke? Our father? Just didn't seem possible. All that energy, all that enthusiasm.

At the edge of Dad's ICU hospital bed, the reality hit me: Dad as I knew him, was gone, snuffed out like a beautiful campfire. Of course his eyes said otherwise. The knowledge that he had been altered lay unfurled in the depths of his pupils.

I miss him today, and in some ways I did actually miss him, as if I'd skipped past and not been seen. I missed him. Or did he miss me? I was the young girl who was never my age. Again I hear him. "Elin is 5, 6, 7, 8 whatever—going on 30." He called me things like "amazing" and "perceptive." I felt invincible as a child.

As puberty stripped me of my girlish features I began to question the earlier accolades bestowed upon me. My approval rating with my father seemingly slipped. My exposure to him was reduced to fleeting moments at the dinner table where I excused myself as soon as my plate was empty. My parents' evening ritual of martinis kept me closed away, and I no longer wanted to hear speeches long since memorized. My father's own professional journey had been derailed, and his preoccupations increasingly ruled his time. I, the last of the Stebbins offspring, sort of disappeared.

Hi E,

Where has the time blown off to? It is already feeling like winter is breathing down our necks. I actually had to scrape frost off my windshield the other morning! I can't even believe that it's Halloween this week. It's on a Friday, yay!!! We are having a really big costume party over at Meadow Wood and it should be a blast. I haven't decided what to dress up as yet but it will probably end up being something easy to put on, yeah, like my waitress uniform! Yuck! Oh well, I'll figure that out later.

Things with Derrick are going great. I love the way he always wants me to be part of everything he does. Sometimes I wish I could just step out of this school life and help him run his firewood business. He also does some masonry work but now that it's getting colder, he and his brother won't have as much of that to do. They just finished a job in Riverside building the most beautiful stone wall. It's hard to believe that such tough men can actually create something of such beauty. You just don't imagine it from looking at them. All the attention to detail, making sure each shape fits with the next and that the colors coordinate, too.

Things are always interesting. So yesterday Derrick and I were driving down the Post Road and a cop pulled us over. I was super freaked out by it but he tells me it happens all the time. He thinks the cops deliberately pick on him.

"License and registration?"

"Sure, officer. Can you tell me why I am being stopped?"

"Well, young man, you have a brake light that's out."

"Really? Thanks, I wasn't aware of that. Is there anything else?"

"That's it, but I need to run your information through the system. Hang tight, I'll be right back." The policeman walked away and Derrick slammed his fist on the steering wheel. I jumped.

"What?" he asked.

"You startled me. It all sounds pretty much like nothing. I mean, it's just a brake light, right?"

"You have no clue, Elin."

"What is that supposed to mean?"

"Look, Elin, I don't mean that in a disrespectful way but believe me when I tell you the Greenwich cops are always out to get me and my brother. It's like a game to them. I swear to God I get stopped at least once a week."

"Really?"

"Yeah, really."

The cop was walking back. I could see him in the side mirror, and Abby was growling.

"That will be all, Mr. Rhoades."

"Thanks officer, you have a great day." You could hear the sarcasm in his voice but the policeman didn't bite the hook.

I keep wondering what that means, "The cops are always out to get me and my brother." Not that I really want to bring it up again, he was obviously not wanting to talk about it yesterday. He got all quiet and I decided to just let it go.

Hi,

Shit, where do I begin? I'm never home. Ugh. The Halloween party was fun last weekend and a ton of people showed up, so many that the cops arrived around midnight. Kevin thinks his grandmother called them (not that I blame her). There was a ton of "contraband," so people were all freaked out about the cops but they really just wanted the majority of the people to "disperse," as they put it. It ended up just about fifteen of us and we partied all night. Not that sleeping would have been an option!

So that was all good, but then we had to go and beam into this week and worse last night.

Last night was so f-d up. Derrick asked me to cut his hair. He had his final foray with the dreadlocks I guess on Halloween. Kind of glad—I mean I didn't totally care but I kind of did. They were sort of, I don't know, gross? Dad took a dim view of them and of course made a jab about them! Anyway, after the shower it was OK, but . . .

Well anyway, he asked me to cut his hair. Of course I said yes and then out of nowhere he had to add that his old girlfriend Rita used to cut it. Like I care? Anyway so we went to his room to cut it, but first I thought maybe I could untangle part of it. (Uh, NO!) Anyway all of a sudden Brett burst through the door and just started in on Derrick.

"You little fucking hippie ass reggae lovin' piece of shit . . . look at you. What's wrong with YOU? What d'ya think . . . your little girlfriend here's gonna untangle it? Then what, huh? You little fucking punk!"

"Brett, buzz off. Elin's cutting my hair. You just don't worry about me, man, it's my hair. I really don't give a shit what you think."

"What are you, some kind of reggae worshipper? Rasta man? Huh,

Derrick, huh??? Talk, you little punk."

"Brett . . . " I started to say.

"Elin, stay out of it," Derrick barked through clenched teeth.

"No, I won't stay out of it. Brett, listen, I'm cutting his hair. Leave him alone."

"Oh, aren't you wonderful, Elin," Brett said in this hideous mocking voice, and then he slammed the door on us.

"What the hell was that all about?" I was kind of shaking. What a jerk . . . I can't imagine anyone in my family talking to each other like that.

"Don't worry about it," Derrick says in his New York accent voice.

"I'm not worried," I lied. "I just can't believe him. What the heck does he have against you?"

"I was born, whatever. He's a prick. Forget about it. Just cut my damn hair, forget the untangling, it ain't happening." OK then.

So I start cutting his hair, and about halfway through I kind of stand back to take a look and I start to laugh. He's got practically no hair on the one side and then all these dreads on the other . . . and on the floor there's all these dreads. It just made me laugh . . . like that laugh when you shouldn't laugh? Yeah.

"Shut the hell up, Elin, it's not fuckin' funny. Just cut my hair already, won't ya?"

"Alright! Jeez, be nice—don't talk to me like that. I'll flippin' cut your hair already! Temper tantrum. What's with everybody tonight? I'm just trying to have fun."

"Yeah, fun." Then in that stupid Archie Bunker voice he says, "Ah jeesh, there girlie, won't ya just cut my hair already?"

The mood passed over but, my God, those Rhoades boys can be so testy.

ABUSIVE BEHAVIOR ERODES a person slowly. Imagine a pair of shoes whose soles are so worn there are holes in each. When they came out of the box fresh and new no one would have imagined their tattered state. Yet over time it happens; they are walked on day in and day out, feet dragged and scuffed, tread marks over pavement, which wears down the layers until one day later they are not recognizable.

Before Derrick, I drove a car and thought I was great at it. I knew my desires as well as any seventeen-year-old could. I loved to laugh. I felt attractive. I made decisions in split seconds. I read great books. I was never afraid to share my opinion. I considered myself bright and interesting—all in all a great catch. Certainly I had my insecurities, my heart had been broken, but I still felt good about being me. I was loved by family and friends, and I am positive I would never have believed that I would fall victim. Ever.

Leo Tolstoy wrote, "Happy families are all alike. Every unhappy family is unhappy in its own way." Is this true of everyone, I wonder, or simply true of those sad families in tragic Russian novels? The world population is roughly 6,882,240,194, but at the split second I write the number it changes. I discover this through a website that uses logarithmic equations obtained through statistical analysis to recalculate constantly while factoring rate of birth and death.

One could surmise that there is an infinite number of ways to define family just based on the knowledge of our world population alone. *Family*— I have turned this word over and over again and it never looks the same. For some, family is a form of incarceration; for others, it is the inception of freedom, confidence, and liberation.

Are we all slowly robbed of our childhoods? My mind traces the silhouettes of each of my own children and I wonder what pieces they are missing. Conversely there are the pieces that *are* there—times that my words cut like a knife, sharp enough to shave a piece of them away. I see it reflected in their expressions. Their eyes bore into me and in that instant—like a flash of a camera—I see them age.

Missing from my own childhood was the freedom to be unencumbered by future greatness. Missing was the freedom to be truly my age—just that, nothing more, nothing less. Flipping through my memories after I was seven, I cannot think of one family gathering where together we were doing something—anything—camping, hiking, biking, playing tennis, a board game. My family memories are of sitting with whomever was home during cocktail hour, followed by dinner table conversations that were always at a rolling boil, and mostly feeling as if I didn't have the admission ticket to join.

My dad was not by nature a violent man. He was, however, capable of delivering blows, particularly to himself—masochistic rants for which he was notorious. "Goddamn it, Stebbins, you *stupid* son of a bitch!" Rants that in retrospect were normal to me. Normalization of self-deprecation left me vulnerable.

Hi,

Brett is acting so weird lately. Ever since the whole haircut incident, it's as if he has a mission to torment everyone. Not so much me really but he picks on Kevin a lot and also Derrick. Obviously it totally irritates me when he picks on Derrick. The smallest of things, too, I don't get it. When I first met him he was so sweet to everyone, maybe because he knew he would need a place to live or something. I have tried to talk to Derrick about it and he just shrugs it off to moodiness.

"Doesn't it bug you? How do you tolerate that out of him? You so don't

deserve to be treated like that, Derrick."

"Yeah, it bugs me, of course, but he's my brother. He's moody. It's not that big of a deal. Believe me I have seen him way worse, I don't want to provoke him."

"What exactly does that mean?"

"Nothing. I just don't really want to draw attention to it, Elin, seriously, he'll snap out of it. He's probably just bummed that work has been slow. He's kind of the type who kicks the dog when he's pissed, only in this case I am the dog."

"You are the dog? You sound sort of OK with that."

"I just don't let it get to me. You've seen him . . . lots of times he's fun to be with. Seriously, it will pass. Don't let it bug you."

"It's hard not to let it bug me, I mean, he picks on Kevin, too. I hate that. Kevin doesn't deserve that and he's gotta share a room with him, too."

"Kevin is just fine, he can hold his own. Elin, you aren't everyone's mom here. Let it go."

"I know, but I care about you guys."

"I know, I know you do. But really, just stay out of Brett's way. It will pass over. Something is obviously eating at him and telling him to knock it off isn't going to make him stop. If anything it will just make him more of a jerk. He is so like my dad."

"Like your dad?"

"Yeah, I don't want to get into it really but to keep it simple, my dad is moody like that, too. Nothing's good enough when he's like that. Anyway, let's think about other stuff . . . like how much I love you."

"Oh, that will solve the world's problems!"

"Not the world's but mine." His whole face is lit up with a smile, so of course I melt.

Hey E,

Derrick took me up to Stamford to meet his mom. She is really sweet. She has an enormous collection of turtles, not live ones, but wood, ce-ramic, stuffed, glass, you name it. She was so happy to meet me and to see

Derrick. He was super uptight the entire time we were there, kept asking her all these questions about her boyfriend and what she is eating and stuff. It was kind of embarrassing for me. He was treating her kind of like a little kid but she didn't seem to care, just answered all of his questions. Later when we left I asked him what all that was about and he started telling me how her boyfriend is a whack job and his mom is a full-on alcoholic and tends to forget to eat. He hates the boyfriend, says the guy is a total asshole and that he sometimes hurts his mother and he plans to kick the guy's head in if he as much as lays another finger on his mom.

His mom didn't seem drunk to me—maybe a little glassy-eyed but not like the stereotype I have in my head, you know, slurring and falling down. It wasn't any of that. If anything she just wanted to make us comfortable and she did not want us to leave at all. Her life seems really sad. She lives in a dumpy apartment in kind of a scary area—well, not scary but uncomfortable.

Derrick has driven me past the house he grew up in and let's just say the apartment is a far cry from her old house. She must feel as if she fell from the top of a really high ladder and smacked her face on every rung coming down to the concrete floor. Sad. The whole thing just makes me sad. I have to say it also makes me feel super appreciative. My family has had its hard knocks but nothing like what I saw today.

I CAN PICTURE my mom's hand, her left hand to be exact, adorned with her own mother's ring. The spectrum of colors that sparkle from the stone scatter around me: purples, yellows, reds—miniscule shards of colored light. This is the engagement ring my grandfather gave to my grandmother, and my own mother inherited it after my grandma died. It is a solitaire diamond from Tiffany's.

In an old sepia-tinted photograph of my grandfather, he has his cigar firmly grasped between the fingers of his left hand. The ash is so long you fear it may fall, perhaps foreshadowing his own future and his plunge from wealth. An insignia ring of some sort, I think Masonic, encircles his pinky. The placement of the ring along with the gripped cigar seem so deliberate, the combination exudes confidence in a way that complements the look in his eyes. My grandmother was his second wife and thirty years his junior. She was petite, with eyes the size of half dollars and skin like porcelain. All the portraits of their family from that time are very formal. He, the attorney turned famous developer of Pelham Heights, New York, also served as congressman to both the sixteenth and twenty-fourth districts off and on for twenty years. Clearly they were accustomed to a life of comfort before the Depression wiped them clean.

Mother's stories of her youth always transfixed me; how I wished we could wind back the clock and visit that home, walk the halls, rooms, and galleries of its impossible size, and finger the tapestries that hung from every window. Each room had a key and she saved them—all skeleton style and each with a story lying dormant in its unpolished metal. These keys recall an era where children were seen and not heard and giggling was forbidden at the dining room table. Despite the formalities, Mother describes her childhood quite happily, her father as a warm and loving man capable of crawling on his hands and knees while carrying his daughters on his back. But in the photos I see a distance that perhaps has wended its way through the generations that followed.

If I could flip up the top of my head and look inside my brain, I would swear that staring back at me would be a sonar device. This hyper-vigilance that I have for each of my kids is always on the lookout for threats. Conversely, on occasion I have an experience that settles me into feeling as if their strength and resilience is insulation from a perpetrator. But I know better and a nagging at the back of my mind insists: abuse doesn't discriminate and anyone can fall victim to it.

I watched a movie with my daughter not long ago, a contrived story about a girl soccer player. In the story the girls soccer team is disbanded at the school but the main character's determination to play the game leads her to attempt to join the boys team; she is turned down. In her frustration she disguises herself as her twin brother (who is conveniently out of the country) and tries out for the soccer team at his school.

I was humbled when Chandler announced to me that she would do the same.

"Really. What makes you think that?"

"Simple, Mom. There is nothing I can't do and I sure as heck won't tolerate being stopped 'cause I'm a girl."

Wow . . . "That is really cool, Chandler. Tell me what else you think about the movie."

"Well, parts of it are *really* stupid, but she is super strong and she doesn't sit on the sidelines and wait for life to happen—she goes out and makes it. She's tough . . . like me."

"You are strong, I admire that in you."

My children are not a reflection of me; they are individuals in their own right. Chandler has a constitution that is different from my own. Almost nothing makes her cry. She smashed into the tetherball pole and her lip swelled—no tears. On the soccer field, she went up against another girl twice her size. Their collision was so intense that they were both sent flying to the ground. The other girl? Sobbing, remains on the ground. Chandler? Springs to her feet ready to go again. Time and time again we see examples of her strength and fortitude.

"Not my daughter, not my sons," my own version of a telepathic plea that slips into the void as a prayer. "Dear God, if you can hear me, please don't allow anything to violate the innocence of my children—not my daughter, not my sons. They are too smart; they know how to make great choices." As soon as the words are released I feel the discomfort that follows when I hear myself relying on a prayer.

I know that it has nothing to do with being smart or stupid, and it has nothing to do with good or bad choices. It is a very slow erosion of self that takes over and leaves a victim doubting everything she ever knew or believed. I shake my head and remind myself that arming my children with information and creating time to hear them is the best way to protect them. Hoping and praying is not a strategy; my utterances feel hollow and even greedy.

Hi,

'Tis the season to be jolly, so then why am I so depressed??? He won't come over for Thanksgiving. What is the big deal?

"I'm not into the family scene."

"What does that mean?"

"What it sounds like . . . not my gig . . . not my thing. It'll be me and Abby on Thanksgiving, thanks but no."

I can only speculate that it's 'cause of how messed up his own family is but I would think he would want to be with me—not just his dog. This is my family, not his. He's met Mom and Dad and Rod, but I want him to meet Paul and Lorna too. John won't be home.

Well, Fergus is coming back home from school in about two weeks, I invited him over for Advent. He said yes. At least he likes being with my family. Mom is always telling me that having things in common with your boyfriend in the way of family is important. I think maybe I am beginning to see her point.

But I love Derrick. I feel sorry for him. It's sad. It's not his fault that his family is all jacked up. Maybe he'll come around and if he comes over then he can see what I mean about my family and how great everyone is.

Hi,

It's Mom's birthday and the second Advent—as it turns out Fergus did make it over. We had the nicest family dinner and again everyone but John was here to celebrate. At one point I was in the kitchen and was singing that Carole King song, "Too Late," and my mom asked me if I was singing the song for Fergus or Derrick. Hmmmmm . . . Of course I snapped, "Neither," and said it in a mean way. But then I remembered it was her birthday and felt bad, and then said something like, "Mom, can I just sing for singing's sake? There is no deep meaning." She just looked at me in that Elinor way . . . you know, the "You aren't fooling me" look. Yeah, so maybe it was for Derrick? Ughhhhh, I don't know, it's so confusing!!!!!

It's like I am still totally in love with Fergus. It's so different. There's no bullshit and his background is so like mine. He's from a big family, too, and his folks are still together. We can really talk.

After dessert, while everyone else was drinking coffee, Fergus and I went out on the Mianus River. It's all frozen over. We walked clear to the dam. The moon was out and it was so beautiful. Everything was so still, had it not been for the crunching of our feet on the snow that covered the ice, the silence would have been deafening. It was super cold, numbing really. Fergus stopped at one point and reached for me and there we stood in each other's arms, his chin perched on my head (the famous private leaning post). Tears were all in my eyes for missing him. Our breath lingered in front of us, whispering of kisses spent. It's all still there—maybe even more so, but we can't . . . I felt the dead end in the stillness and wished I could halt time from moving forward.

He's at school in Vermont, I'm down here. Derrick . . . it's so perplexing. How can I love them both? They are SO different. I feel so much more myself around Fergus, he just loves me and lets me be me. In my mind's eye I can still see him standing outside Alex's parents' front door having returned within moments of leaving. With a grin opening the glass door I whispered, "Miss me already?"

With a yes nod he said, "Thank you."

"Thank you? For what? Do you want to come back in?" I ask him.

"No . . . no need, I gotta go. BUT, thank you for just being you. I really, really love you."

Poof, he was gone—with that long-legged dash down the stairs.

And here I am in my room and the tears are blinding me as I write . . . yeah, poof and he is gone, only this time for good. "Thank you for being you." Who am I? Am I the me with Fergus, the me with Derrick, the me with my girlfriends?

Hi.

It's Christmas day . . . not even a phone call from Derrick.

GOING, GOING, GONE—poof. Compared with geological time, a childhood is over as fast as blowing out the candles on a birthday cake. What do they wish for as their eyelashes meet their cheeks? I know what I wish for—their happiness, safety, and comfort. Does wishing make it so? I feel my head shake no almost involuntarily and the truth settles over me. I must keep my eyes open, be present. What I do, how I respond, the way I listen, seeing them as they are—all these things serve them. After all, they didn't ask to be born but were born anyway—a line my own father was famous for, and right he was. I contend that children, once they are here, simply want to be loved. They want to be recognized for their own unique qualities. First they want that recognition to come from their parents; later that recognition comes from within.

When my sister was three, she had a recurring nightmare. She was in the dark, but she could see her hands and they were holding an enormous roll of toilet paper, only it was disappearing rapidly. She knew she had to get to my parents—either one of them—before it was gone otherwise something terrifying would happen. The dream surfaced after the death of our brother and my parents' first-born son, Robbie. In another dream she would try to tell herself to wake up only she couldn't. While in it she was required to walk through every room of a house as if taking inventory—but she didn't know why. He was gone, and really she doesn't remember anything other than the dreams and the fact that she was terrified of doctors for a long time after.

While I was little, my sister checked in often and always made me feel she was there for me. She is the one who saved all my mementoes: scraps of written notes, drawn pictures. She collected them for my future self—it's as if she knew someday I would want the evidence that many years ago I was a little girl.

She was so young when Robbie died . . . he disappeared. I imagine her in her dreams walking through the enormous New England house, going from room to room—a three-year-old's inventory, perhaps looking for what no longer was there to find.

The ridgeline of this family scar is broad; only the fingertip can detect the meandering lasso-like path that carved its way from Massachusetts, where my mother, phone in hand, reached Alaska where my father stood listening. Dad was in the wilderness when he learned his child, a son he would never have the opportunity to hold, was fighting for his life. I try to picture him absorbing the information. Was he in shock? Were the fundamental differences between the way they each related to anything personal at play? His response would fuel anger and resentment in his wife and simultaneously serve as a vehicle to prove to him that his innate distrust of women was warranted. His response was abysmal: "What do you want me to do?"

Later, he stepped away from those words, got on a plane, and together with my mother buried their child. Then he went back to work and my mother was left to hold together their fractured family, with no time to grieve fully.

As a grown woman I feel tenderness for her that I have difficulty expressing. There was no guidebook to get her through. In a way, that connects us . . . each of us has forged our own path out of darkness and into the light.

Hi E,

New Year's was a blast. All of us partied at Meadow Wood. It was so much fun! In addition to our Meadow Wood hodgepodge of Mark, Brett, Kevin, Derrick, and me, Derrick's friend Drew came over with Mike and we drank beers all night. Kelli showed up later in the evening, which was nice for me (something besides trucks, motorcycles, and odd jobs to talk about). It was perfect to hang without a million people. Drew is a great guy; he decided to move back in with his parents so no doubt we will be seeing way more of him. He's hoping Janet, his girlfriend, will move to Connecticut also. That freaks me out some; she was really good friends with Rita, Derrick's old girlfriend, who lately I have to hear about all the time like she was some goddess. Drives me nuts, Rita this, Rita that. I'm sure she is a great person but I really don't want to talk about her all the time. Or hear about how wonderful she is for that matter. Anyway, New Year's, it was fun.

Fergus left, back to school for him. I guess I am kind of relieved; it was not easy having him home, but not really having him. I guess also it made Derrick seem somehow all wrong for me when he was here. In some ways I actually almost felt I was outside looking in. But now I feel better about him, like I am inside again. Weird. Whatever that really means . . .

———

Hi E,

OK, you are never going to believe this!!!!!!!

I am right now at this moment living with Kelli in Port Chester! It's not permanent or anything, Jack left for the races in Daytona with Derrick and Brett so he asked her to stay at his place for him and since there is an extra room she asked me to stay with her too. I can't even believe Mom said yes. I sold her on the fact that Kelli shouldn't be alone and Port Chester is actually *closer to school than Riverside where my parents now live. This is so cool. Kelli and I are planning to party!*

Derrick has no idea—all this happened right after he left. The guys are going to be gone something like two weeks. I am kinda glad he is gone for a while. He has been really possessive lately, constantly on me about who I am hanging out with at school, and who I talk to at the restaurant where I waitress. Oh my God! I am like, What??? What do you want to know? Who I talk to? Puhlease!!! He can be so flippin' jealous—like I would cheat on him! Everyone in this town knows I am his girlfriend. Most people have no interest in messing with the Rhoades brothers. I highly doubt anyone's gonna make a move on me. Oh yeah, perfect example: about two weeks ago we were in Lou's and Hunter Blazedale came in with David Mortimer. OK, I admit I dated David, but Derrick doesn't even know that. He says to me, I don't like the way that Hunter guy looks at you. Hunter?! He can be so stupid sometimes. I just kind of stared at him like he had five heads or something. I mean I did sleep with Hunter, but just once. Hardly anyone even has a clue about it. Well David does hence the end of that. Way too complicated. Anyway, I have never intentionally given Derrick a reason to be jealous. I suppose there is an attraction with Hunter, but it's not like what Derrick thinks. I mean Hunter and I have known each other for so long. Seriously, we would have already gone there when we had the chance. Didn't happen and it left us to be buddies. Anyway, Derrick is just jealous about anything. Can you imagine if he knew about Fergus? He would die.

Some feelings are best left deep down inside, you know, like in a strong box? It needs a key but it's fireproof and everything inside remains safe. In some ways I don't even let myself in there, why would I let him in?

I hate the double standard, too. He gets in my face about who I talk to yet he runs off at the mouth about Rita the Madonna. Do I get all pissy? Not to his face. Writing helps. I don't want to think about this! I am here in PC, with Kelli. We are going to The Roadside tonight for drinks and what more do I need to think about. We know all the bouncers at The Roadside so it's not like we'll have to wait to get in. Maybe I'll actually see some of my friends. I haven't been out in forever!

Hmmm . . .

Hi E,

Ugh, it's really early on a Sunday morning and I cannot even believe who just left the apartment. Yeah . . . maybe I need to start at the beginning.

So last night Kelli and I go to The Roadside (Yeah, like that's something new). Anyway, she was on a roll, working the room with people like Chris and Ray but I was kind of feeling mellow so I took a seat at the bar and ordered a beer. I'm just chilling out when I start to scan the bar to see who else is here. No one I know. Then I see this guy at the other end of the bar staring at me. I actually looked behind me I am so not used to having people stare at me 'cause I am with Derrick 98 percent of the time. Yeah, no one behind me. I look back and he breaks into this huge smile as if to say, "I am looking at you." I smile back but then look down 'cause I really don't even know what to do. The next thing I know he's walking toward me. Great, now what? He slides up alongside me and says something like, "Hey my name's Pete." I smile and don't reply and he says "That's when you say, 'Hi, Pete, my name's . . . '" I shake my head in embarrassment and say, "OK, I can do that. Hi, Pete, my name's Elin. Anything I should add?" He shakes his head no and then says, "Elin, did I get that right? E-Lynn." I nod. "So, Elin, wanna get high?" Hmmm. Yeah, let's see, you're gorgeous and I am totally unsure what or why me . . .

"Sure." I look around for Kelli. She's still hanging with Chris, so I give her the wave that means "Be right back" and out we go. We cruise across the lot to a slightly obscure area but not so much that we are completely hidden. He lights up and inside I am thinking about how I hardly ever smoke anymore. Well, I take a hit and it's just gross, some homegrown rag weed or some kind of garbage like that, I notice it's already partly smoked and now I am kind of over being outside but, I'm cool, we hang not saying too much. Then out of nowhere the guy, this Pete, leans in to kiss me. I brush him away. "Look, Pete, this is a quick smoke. I'm not into kissing you." He tries again and the alarm bell goes off in my head. I back away and say, "I said I'm not into kissing you, buddy." Well, then the asshole pushes me up against the flippin' dump truck I was standing next to and proceeds to try to ram his entire tongue down my throat! I was so pissed!!! With both hands I shove the jerk off of me and yell, "Listen, you asshole, I said no, so get the fuck off me!" I somehow manage to kick him in the leg, too, and as I am

trying to get away from the jerk I catch my coat on some bar thing sticking up on the dump truck and totally rip it. I was so pissed. "Who the fuck do you think you are? Jeez you are a jerk!" I am sprinting at this point away from him back to the bar. I hear him stammering some lame thing about me, like cock tease or whatever. Oh my God, like I owe him anything.

So back in the bar I can't find Kelli. Great. I'm scanning the whole place when my eyes land on Hunter. "There's welcome company," I think as I head over to the table he is at alone. So, maybe I wasn't the most sober person in the room but Hunter was drunk, beyond smashed. He starts telling me how he needs to get home. "Shut up," I say to him, still leaning on my leftover anger from the Pete incident. "I am so not letting you drive." I have spent countless nights at the Blazedale's house in backcountry Greenwich playing pool and there is no way I am letting him drive from PC all the way home. "DON' WORRY 'BOUT IT!" he yells. Yeah, right, so it's not even worth my ink to describe the stupid conversation we had about him not driving, if I could only write in slurs. Talk about an idiot! Finally I drag his half-conscious butt out of The Roadside and we walk back to the apartment. So we pass out, yeah he slept in the bed, but trust me I did not touch him or him me. I wake up this morning and just about have a heart attack thinking about what Derrick would say/do if he saw this. Of all people, Hunter! I am just lying there staring at him when slowly his eyes open. I always forget about his eyes until I am looking at them. Those huge blue eyes. "Elin, Elin, Elin." His face breaks into a smile that looks like it's masking a head-banging headache.

"How ya feeling, Hunter?"

"Yeah . . . I didn't . . . you know . . . try . . ."

"No, no, nothing like that. You were hammered and remember, I have a boyfriend. Not going there again with you."

"Yeah . . . " We hung out for maybe fifteen minutes and he was looking greener by the minute and then he's on his way out with words about how much I saved his ass from the stupid Greenwich cops and his parents' wrath . . . yeah, whatever . . . "I guess you're worth it," I laugh at him.

Kelli walks into my room as soon as he's out the door on foot for The Roadside to get his truck. "It's not what you think," I say in response to the huge shit-eating grin on her face. "Seriously, it was nothing, he was drunk— beyond driving . . . you know, he doesn't exactly need a DWI."

"Sure, E."

I know she's just messing with me. We laugh about what Derrick would do, but inside I feel that knife-like pain in my gut. Just thinking about him coming back makes me cringe a little. I miss him, but Kelli and I have been having so much fun! All the guys should be back Monday or Tuesday, which will mean I am back at my parent's house! Ugh.

I can't wait for spring break, it feels like eternity till it will be here. School is dragging along right now. I am working on putting an art show together, so that's cool. A few of the other kids want to put their work in the show too. Should be good.

Hi there.

What a messed up afternoon. I feel like I did when I was six and I lost Mom at the department store and started crying and some lady helped me find her, only there is no one helping me right now.

Derrick got home from Florida and he is super pissed off that I stayed with Kelli. What? What's up with that? It's like he's in an argument with himself but pushes it on me.

"You think you can just do whatever you want? Huh? Answer me! Huh?"

"What are you talking about? Yeah, I can do what I want. What the hell crawled up your ass? I thought you'd be happy! I actually thought you would think it was great."

"Yeah, maybe you should stop thinking. Don't want to hurt yourself or anything."

"What?"

"You heard me."

"I'm out of here. Up yours!"

"Fine." He kind of started kicking the ice on the driveway and I was feeling like the tears were coming on. I started to walk away.

"Wait."

"What?!"

"OK, this really isn't what I thought would happen when I saw you. All the

time down in Daytona I couldn't stop thinking about you up here in Green-wich and I just missed you so much but it makes me crazy to think of you going out with Kelli and just . . . I don't know . . . having guys hit on you."

"Guys hitting on me? Right. What is it with you . . . it's like you just don't trust me."

"No, it's not you. I know . . . I know . . . it's Rita . . . "

"Derrick, look, I am not Rita. The room's too small for her to be here . . . and we are outside." *Now I am crying Ugh, I hate when I cry, it's like every-thing just falls apart.*

"I am so sick of Rita and I don't even know her!"

"You're right . . . I know you're right." *More driveway scuffing.*

"What? There's something else—what?"

"I just don't think Kelli is the best person for you to hang out with."

"Derrick, don't go there with me, you aren't my dad and here's a news-flash for you, he wouldn't say that either! Kelli is my friend. I mean, really, I don't see half of my friends 'cause I am always with you."

"Elin, I just love you so much, I missed you—even Abby missed you. I just can't even imagine what I would do without you. I would be a wreck." *Now he has tears in his eyes. We hug . . . I feel suffocated.*

"I'm not going anywhere, I promise. Can we just start over?"

So that's what we did. We pretended to rewind the clock and said stu-pid things like "Wow, you're back from Florida," and "Cool, you stayed with Kelli," all really put on, you know, like a one-act play or something. Of course we then slept together. I had to go. I just felt so helpless after . . . as if the bed sheets had strangled me or something. I watched him smoke his cigarette and all the smoke was kind of around his head and I felt like cry-ing again. I pushed myself up to get dressed and he began to protest and I just told him Mom was expecting me back home for dinner and I needed to get going. He started to apologize again and I said it was OK. "No big deal" is what I think I said. But now I am sitting here and that helpless and little feeling drove all the way home with me. Even the really hot shower didn't help.

THERE WAS A time where I tried to wipe my memories of Derrick from my memory bank. Those toxic years were like a long bout of food poisoning—shaking, fever, can't hold your bowels, projectile vomiting, dehydrated delirium, wishing for recovery or death. Despite all the purging, deep down there's no forgetting. Life doesn't work that way.

There were triggers—someone would say or do something that would set off an automatic physical response, like trembling. A gesture as simple as someone removing a stray hair from my eyes would cause me to flinch.

When Jimmy and I were first together, he tickled me, and for a split second I felt like he was trapping me. I flipped out, and that is how he learned that bruises don't always heal on the inside. Loud voices and any threat of a physical conflict make me tremble and my palms sweat.

My life has been shaped by my survival, and allowing what I endured to settle into my marrow has infused me with a strength that will not waver. Abuse had an effect on me, but it has not made my life any less worthy, any less important, or any less valuable. I refuse to walk around leaning on that experience like a pair of crutches. I am not damaged goods, I am me.

Hi.

It was really bugging me the whole thing that happened, so I told Derrick we had to talk about it more. I pretty much told him his jealousy was really getting on my nerves and I couldn't handle it. I also told him the Rita thing had to stop. I am me, not her. He actually seemed to really get it. He told me that she really burned him, left him for some other guy, and it really messed him up, he'd trusted her. I guess I get it, I told him, but I am not that person and he had to stop treating me like I was or I couldn't be with him. That seemed to wake him up. He was pretty emotional . . . started telling me how I really get him and he's never been able to talk to anyone about his parents and stuff. It was a really good conversation. He told me his dad was really rough on his mom.

"You know, you met my mom. She even lives with a similar prick now."

"Derrick, look, I know you don't like your mom's boyfriend but I don't get what that has to do with us."

Long silence . . .

"Derrick? What?"

"My mom called last night. That jerk of a boyfriend slapped her around. So she calls me, I drive up there, the asshole's gone. My mom is hammered. It was a mess. I can't deal. What does she expect me to do?"

In my head I am thinking something like "You have got to be kidding me . . . what kind of life is that?" but instead I continue to quiz him.

"Why didn't you say something before?"

"'Cause you were on my case about my jealousy and Rita. I mean I get that, I just . . . I don't know . . . Elin, look, I am sorry, you have to believe me. I think it's just that you are really the only person that is important to me."

"Other people are important. Look, you were just talking about your mom. She is important."

"She's a drunk. Seriously, she can hardly manage and when shit happens *she expects me to just come save the day? I mean what am I supposed to do? Drive all over looking for that prick hoping I can find him? You should have seen her, crying, and all hysterical about how she can't take it anymore."*

"That must have made you feel so horrible."

"Yeah, it did. There's not a thing I can really do. She'll end up killing herself from drinking if that asshole doesn't kill her first."

"Don't say that!"

"Elin, you are so . . . sheltered. I mean, I love that about you. But sometimes I think you see the world through serious rose-colored glasses."

"Well, I like my view."

He was really upset. I felt so sad for him. I can't imagine my dad hitting Mom. Obviously that's why Brett is the way he is. Derrick really needs me, it's so sad. I wish I could just wave a magic wand and make all his pain disappear along with the memories he must have rolling through his mind.

———

Hi.

What a completely fucked up afternoon. I was over at Meadow Wood and we were all in the kitchen having our usual beers. It was me, Derrick, Mark, and Kevin, just totally chilling out having a fine time, and in walks Brett. I could tell from the second he walked through the door that he was in a foul mood; he seemed semi-drunk and just on edge or something. Derrick was sitting to my right and Kevin and Mark were on the other side of the table. Brett walks up behind Derrick and just hovers over his shoulder. Derrick turns around and asks him if he has a problem. That question sucked all the air out of the room. You could hear a pin drop, even Abby got up and went into the other room.

Then it was like an explosion . . .

"What's my problem? WHAT'S MY PROBLEM? I don't know, Derrick, what's MY problem. Let me think about that. OH, that's it. YOU'RE MY FUCKING PROBLEM!"

Derrick started to turn around like he was going to stand up and Brett pushed him down into his chair. Derrick kind of ducked down and I stood up so fast that my chair fell over. Then Brett just starts beating the shit out of

Derrick. Derrick was trying to get up and Brett kept hitting him back down. I am screaming at him to stop it. Mark and Kevin were on their feet just watching.

"DO SOMETHING, YOU GUYS!!!!!!! BRETT, STOP IT, LEAVE HIM ALONE . . . STOP . . . "

I start yanking on his shirt, trying to get him off of Derrick while Mark and Kevin do jack shit to help me. All of a sudden Brett whips around and flippin' backhands me across the face.

"WHAT THE FUCK IS YOUR PROBLEM?" I am beyond rational at this point. I am crying and just a mess and he starts pushing me with his fingertips pressed onto my shoulders.

"How old are you, little girl? Huh? What, seventeen? Huh? Does your mommy know where you are? Huh, my problem? You are all my problem," he tells the room with his teeth clamped shut. Then he picks up the chair that I had knocked over and breaks it into pieces and storms out.

Derrick is all eyes down on the floor. I am shaking uncontrollably and crying really hard. Slowly Derrick puts his arm around me . . . or tries to. I move away from his touch and say to all of them, "What the hell? A little help? What is wrong with you guys? Derrick, he may be your brother but that's not right—that's totally screwed up."

Kevin started cleaning up and he kind of looked at me like he was really sorry. Then he says to me, "Hey, Elin, can you help me bring this stuff outside?" I look down at the broken chair and say, "Sure." So once outside with chair parts safely tucked by the trash can, Kevin says to me, "Look, Elin, my grandmother is really losing it with all the partying and everything. They don't know it but she's shutting this thing down hard. Brett's a psycho, both those Rhoades boys are screwed up. You're like a sweet girl . . . I don't get it."

"Kevin, look, I know you're trying to help but Derrick is different from Brett, he's got his issues but he is mostly really sweet to me. I think it will be good to make everyone move, especially for you, get that prick Brett out of your room."

"Yeah, he's a real asshole." Poor Kevin, he's a good guy, he really actually does seem to have a big heart. We head back inside and Mark and Derrick are sitting in the remaining chairs acting like nothing happened. Derrick looks up at me. "Are you OK?"

"Sure, I'm flippin' great. No, I'm not OK, your jerk of a brother hit me. Did you miss that or something?!"

"No, I saw. I am so sorry." Now he's on his feet, and he touches my face. "It's a little red but I doubt it will bruise."

"Oh, that's a plus! I'm sure that would go over great with my family. Ugh, what an asshole!"

Not much later Drew walks through the door. He was beyond incensed over Brett's hitting me. He was telling Derrick if Brett was his brother and Brett hit Janet he would have kicked the ever-living crap out of him. Derrick just stared at the floor, shaking his head. Drew looked at me and it was like he was trying to say something with his eyes but couldn't. I finally left. I'm sitting here on my bed just numb—I can't stop re-playing that psycho scene in my head.

I look around and notice Little and Helpless sitting on my bed next to me again. I slap the space next to me in anger and bark to the air, "I AM NOT HELPLESS AND LITTLE!"

I feel really sorry for Derrick. I just cannot even imagine anyone in my family ever hitting anyone. It's all wrong. He looked so sad when I said good-bye to him tonight. It must really suck to have a family that's fractured like they are.

DERRICK'S BROTHER BORE into him like a drill and sucked him dry of any confidence he may have been born with. His insecurities manifested themselves in need rendering him permanently parched.

Some people reinforce human spirit while others simply rob it. My sister and brothers each deposited droplets of their belief in me into my emotional cistern. It became a container so deep and so full that one would think nothing could siphon confidence from its depths. In many ways I was programmed to believe I could do anything.

I recall days many years ago when I was younger and enveloped in my siblings' love.

"Now I know there's no Easter Bunny . . . "

"What?"

"I saw Mom and Grandma. They were putting candy in the baskets . . . and so I know now." We are standing in the middle of the long hall in our Houston house. Rodger is staring at me, listening intently. I can't keep his gaze and I search the floor in an effort to hold back the tears that are threatening to leak.

"Oh, you didn't hear?"

"Hear what?"

"The Easter Bunny called, and she asked Mom to help her out this year." He doesn't miss a beat. "I bet if I sing you a song, you'll feel better."

"The Easter Bunny can make phone calls?"

"Well, yeah, what'd ya think?"

We are now shuffling toward my room and I am turning over the idea of a rabbit with a telephone receiver up to her long ear. "How does she hold the phone?" I ask as I climb into my bed. He reaches to help me with the covers and all at once I am draped in white cotton. The moon is streaming through my window and lights up the room.

"Check out the moon," Rodger says. We both look up at it floating in the sky on its solo mission to illuminate the dark.

"Do you want me to sing?"

"Well, sure . . . "

Rodger's melodic voice is like an added blanket of comfort. His singing, about the Little Moon way up in the sky, encircles me. Thoughts of the Easter Bunny are safely tucked away, replaced by the love that my brother always exudes.

"E?"

I hear Lorna's voice but I am in that deep, groggy sleep that only occurs just before the dawn.

"E?" Now she's rubbing my back. "Elin, it's time. Remember, the sunrise?"

I do remember and I am thrilled. With the vigor only a small child can produce I roll over and cast away the blanket of warmth and dreams.

"I'm ready!"

"Shhhh." In spite of the dark I can see my sister's finger up against her smiling mouth. She isn't mad; she almost sounds giddy herself.

"Oh, sorry, I'm ready!" I say in a whisper. "Is anyone else awake?"

"No, I think they're all still sleeping."

"Good, it's just you and me, right?"

"Just you and me. Tell you what, you get some clothes on, go the bathroom, and then come to my room and we'll go. Sound good?"

"Yeah! Oh sorry, yeah."

"It's OK, you're excited, but try to be extra quiet when you come find me, OK?"

"OK." I dress in the clothes I had laid out the night before so I could be fast. I grab the present I have for her and with great exaggeration tiptoe to the bathroom and then again to find her at the other end of the house.

"Hey, you look ready!" She is talking normal now and I am relieved that the whispering is over.

"I *am*!" We creep out into the pitch dark driveway and climb into my sister's little car. As soon as the car is in motion I feel as if my babyhood is behind me. Glancing back, I imagine her in the driveway waving me into my future. Later we park where there is an unobstructed view of the horizon and I hand her the picture I painted for her.

"Oh, thanks, E, this is wonderful. I love it."

Surrounded by the majesty of the morning we sit in the quiet and watch while Texas stretches her beautiful pink, yellow, and red streamers across the sky in a show that, I'm sure, is put on just for us.

For Paul, leaving Dobbs House Diner has a jukebox ritual. I watch as he feeds the quarters into the glowing machine and selects *the* song. We both instantly smile when the familiar music breaks into the packed restaurant.

He nods with his farewell grin to the cook while Elton John slides into his refrain for "Honky Cat," and Paul sings along. We slip out the door and into the warm air of the Texas night. As is also his habit, Paul sings the words he knows and alternates with a hum where he doesn't, all the way to the car.

Once inside the car, we are enveloped by the stillness. He looks at me with his keys still in his hand and says, "E-Babes." Then he switches his gaze and attention to starting the car. I watch as he shifts into reverse and turns to back the car out of the parking spot. "E-Babies," he says almost as if to himself but this time with a hint of unadulterated adoration.

A cocoon of quiet envelopes us. I look out the car window and watch the Houston suburbs soar by. There on the seat uncoiled between us is the endless invisible chord of love that will stretch out over a lifetime, defy geography, and serve to remind us that by the soul we will remain forever connected.

My brother John and I are coming home from who knows where when we arrive on our street.

"Alright, it's your turn."

"Huh? What do you mean 'my turn'?"

The motor of the car goes quiet and I stare at John across the center console, we are parked at the top of Shore Acre Drive and no one is in sight.

"Your turn to drive."

"*Drive?* You're kidding, right?"

"Miss Boob, would I ever kid you about that?"

His words register and I can feel my palms break into a cold sweat. He's not kidding.

"OK . . . " I say to his legs, which are the only visible thing to me now since he has climbed from the driver's seat to the street. "Here goes nothing," I say more to myself as I push open the door.

John is always there for me, ready to take on the world; after all it's just the two of us at home now, everyone else is either at school or living on their own. We, the last of the tribe, are sticking together. He smiles at me as I pull myself out of the passenger seat. I feel his penetrating eyes follow me around the back of the car until we meet inside once again in our new places.

"So, first let's talk about what you are going to do."

"Dr. Beard turns into Dr. *Official!*"

He disregards the name-calling because we have forever called each other Miss Boob and Dr. Beard, so much so that it is rare that either of us utter a first name.

He patiently lists all the features of the car, describes in perfect detail what will happen when I turn the key, and finishes by telling me what I need to be aware of. Driving lesson complete, and now it's time. I turn the key and the motor roars to life. Repeating the instructions out loud I put the car into drive and slowly pull back into the street. At the pace of a tortoise we make our way down the street, turn onto Bryon Road and, voila! I, Elin aka Miss Boob, have safely parked the car in our driveway.

"See? Nothing to it. You, Miss Boob, now know how to drive!" I am beaming. As we make our way into the house I feel as if I can do anything, conquer the greatest feat, and stomp out any potential fear. I can drive and there will be no turning back.

Yet despite the abundance of love, despite the outpouring of belief in my abilities, despite the confidence I had accrued, I was vulnerable—vulnerable in a way that allowed my abuser to slowly get a hold of me. He crossed my line and landed squarely on my unsuspecting back. Perhaps part of that confidence was entwined with the will to help others. Did I simply want to save Derrick even at the risk of losing myself? In the end I do not believe that any of it was conscious; after all I was not the one with the power or the control. Put simply, I merely had the desire to make Derrick whole and the confidence to think that I could do it. What I didn't understand was it was a feat that no one could have accomplished but himself.

I twirl this around in my mind. Some people suck you in; they have no desire whatsoever to truly make changes. They place blame, refuse to look inside, and in the end expect others to solve their problems or let them off the hook. There is no helping someone who is unwilling to first help themselves.

Hi E,

As Kevin predicted, his grandmother shut down Meadow Wood. I feel the most sorry for Kevin himself; she is moving to Nebraska so he has to move back with his mom. That's not going to be an easy step for him.

As for the Rhoades brothers, Derrick is moving in with Logan Mallard. He lives right off of Greenwich Avenue in an old house that's been converted into a few apartments. I don't know Logan that well but he seems super nice. I am just glad that Derrick doesn't have to live with Brett!

I have no idea where Brett is moving and truthfully I really don't care. He has not uttered one word to me since he hit me. Kelli tells me that he had a crush on me and that he can't handle his brother having something he doesn't. A crush on me? I doubt it. Not having what his brother has, that is probably closer to the truth. Derrick has love in his life, that probably drives Brett insane. Brett has his dog Ella. I have never known him to have a girlfriend but with his twisted sense of humor and horrible temper, who in their right mind would want to be with him? That dog is a saint—the things I have seen him do to her are appalling. It's weird because he doesn't hit her but he does weird stuff like "body slams," where he jumps on her but somehow keeps his weight from crushing her and then he puts his teeth up close to her face and growls. She just cowers, she is such a sweetie pie, and he is a sadistic asshole. Nothing he does lasts very long and he apologizes to her and hugs her but who cares about the apologies it doesn't change what he did. I just am so glad that I don't have to see him almost every day. The tension between us sucked! He talked to everyone in the room and pretty much acted like I didn't exist. The guy behaves like a two-year-old.

In some ways I will miss Meadow Wood. It's more about the place than anything, the long driveway that winds its way up the hill slowly revealing that enormous house. The property line is thick with trees and amazingly you can't see the house next door.

Hi!

Derrick is moved into Logan's place. It's kind of dumpy especially compared to Meadow Wood, but hey—no Brett! Logan's cool. His girlfriend lives with him, too; she's quiet but seems really nice. The location is good—you know close to stores. The restaurant is just up the street too so that makes it easy when my shift is over. Derrick seems happier, not so heavy from all the crap with Brett, so that's really good, too.

Hey E,

Things are so much better!!!!! I had no idea how much not seeing Brett was going to help Derrick and me. He's always in a good mood, finding a ton of work, and has been doing way more side jobs with Drew instead of his dumb brother. Right now they have a huge job in Riverside re-building a wall. Money helps. I know a month ago Derrick had to ask his dad for money, which really didn't go over very well. I said he should ask his grandfather, that man is the sweetest! Derrick said no, his grandfather is taken care of by his dad so that wouldn't work. Now it's not that big of a deal 'cause he has his own money.

No two fingerprints are alike and each parent leaves his or her own impression when shaping a child's life. My own parents' prints on my upbringing are indelibly stamped into my gestures, perspective, insecurities, confidence, and humility. We all have pieces inside that resemble what has been given and received, conversely there are also those pieces that are missing. That missing piece is spotlighted by what manifested as my own longing, my own need, my own loss.

As the youngest of five I was raised as much by my siblings as by my parents. There was a sense of belonging in my family—*Stebbinsness*. All of us knit together like one of our grandmother's blankets: rich with color, warm but itchy, too, a prelude to growing up and the natural separation of children and parents.

When my father left home to head to college, my grandfather saw my father as his successor. Dad got into MIT, his own father's alma mater. His major would be nautical engineering; he intended to join in the family business, the managing of a shipyard. But when Dad arrived at school, he took an elective in geology that derailed his father's plan. From there he sliced himself from the hold that his parents had on him. My father saw his future and his own father saw a boy skipping after a dream.

It has occurred to me that Dad was robbed of his childhood in ways that I can only guess at. Some stories he shared, but there was more unfiltered truth in what he kept hidden. He once wrote a kind of personal manifesto that he later referred to as "The Fourteen Points." It is set up like a memorandum to an unnamed committee.

My eyes are drawn to points 5, 6, 7, and 9.

> 5. *A human has no control over being born; i.e., he did not and cannot ask to be here. (The recognition of this fact may preclude smugness.)*

This was the starting gun for his sermonlike monologue. I can see him as if the dining room table were in front of me. Dad is at the head of the table, using hand gestures for emphasis. "When you couldn't ask and didn't ask to be born but were *born anyway . . .*"

> 6. *A human possesses qualities described as instinct, talent, reason, intuition, and humor, the intensities of which vary between individuals.*

> 7. *A human does* not *possess qualities described as love, beauty, integrity, conscience, and humility; these are qualities of the universe to which*

To: Those who were not allowed to be children

From: Robert H. Stebbins

Subject: Reflections: intermittent from June 7, 1970 to date

1. Throughout the universe the most fundamental quality and only constant is change; there are no other absolutes and, therefore, there are no ultimates.

2. Ideas can be equated to the product of knowledge multiplied by reason expressed as a power function of intuition; e.g., $I = KR^n$, where I=ideas, K=knowledge, R=reason, n=intuition.

3. The life process thermodynamically is an open system in which entropy is cyclic. (One of the manifestations of the life process is the development of the nuclides.)

4. There is an optimum size (but not fixed) for all organized matter and all organizations of matter.

5. A human has no control over being born; i.e., he did not and cannot ask to be here. (The recognition of this fact may preclude smugness.)

6. A human possesses qualities described as instinct, talent, reason, intuition, and humor, the intensities of which vary within and between individuals.

7. A human does not possess qualities described as love, beauty, integrity, conscience and humility; these are qualities of the universe to which a person responds with or without affection, pleasure, loyalty, guilt and confidence, respectively, depending upon the individual's acceptance of the freedom to do so.

8. Freedom for man comprises doing what he wants when he wants to and being responsible for his actions. The energetics of human want are sustained by sharing, learning and humor and are extinguished by boredom.

9. Basic to man's nature is the endeavor to share, which, if successful, precludes loneliness, arrogance and being devious; friendship is based on mutual sharing; trust is the recognition of when an individual does not threaten another by sharing; fear is the hiatus between the act of sharing and the establishment of trust; "hurt" results from the rejection of one human by another with whom friendship has been established; pride for a human is the recognition of self-confidence (resulting from behavior without contradiction); sensitivity is the ability to share such pride.

10. A human has the propensity to possess wonder (the desire to learn) and knowledge (that which is learned), each of which vary depending upon the responses to the individual's environment that occur as a result of the development of his intuition, talent and reason; wonder is modulated by maturity (the discrimination in the selection of what to learn) and knowledge is modulated by experience (the response to the use of that which is learned).

11. Decisions are demanded by human want; just decisions are those that require behavior without contradiction and their fulfillment depends upon the timing of their execution. (Time is a concept developed by man to "keep track of" change.)

12. Behavior without contradiction is the basis of "morality"; the exceptions to such behavior constitute human reality and are the cause of the need for justice (receipt of the fairest possible reward or penalty for man's actions, regardless of the cause or need for such a determination.)

13. Change also precludes the concepts of "should", "good" and "bad" and "right" and "wrong", except in the context of policy (a declaration that establishes the environment in which procedures either are intended or are instructed to be carried out, as well as the procedures to be followed upon the occurrence of and during specified activities and situations, especially those of major significance and of a recurring nature). "Good" policies allow the opportunity to accomplish what "should" (consensus reached after the consideration of the current pertinent and reliable data) be done by following the "right" (noncontradictory) procedures (statements of the actions to be taken in order to fulfill the intents of policies and for performing specified work). The establishment of policies and the procedures that result from them requires communication (the transfer of information between people such that comprehension is achieved through sanctioned consideration of current pertinent and reliable data: if action is required, the nature of and the authority and responsibility for such action are established).

14. Thinking is aided by remembering to:

    a. Determine assumptions (provisional statements about conditions of significance and consequence in relation to specified activities and over the validity of which little or no control can be exercised; and the likelihood of such present conditions continuing or such future conditions occurring).

    b. Look for contradictions (their recognition provides another opportunity to learn).

    c. Carry any problem to its absurd extreme in either "direction" in order to gain perspective of the problem "as it is".

    d. Recognize that the quality of decisions can be consistently no better than the quality of the data upon which they are based.

a person responds with or without affection, pleasure, loyalty, guilt, and confidence, respectively, depending on the individual's acceptance of the freedom to do so.

I think he truly believed that we were not "his" in the traditional sense; in his own words we were "products of the universe." As a child, I wanted him to be like the fathers of my friends—easygoing, sports-car-driving, office-going, tickle-producing dads. I couldn't fathom as a young girl what it meant to be a "product of the universe." I just wanted him to acknowledge that he was mine and I was his. I had a friend then whose dad brought her to the office, and she would work on projects that were within her ability. His belief in her has stood the test of time, and today she is an integral part of the family business. When you're growing up, it's hard not to compare a friend's life to your own. I could see dads who were doing things with their daughters, who had conversations with them, who were physical with them. I saw dads who skied with their daughters, took them to hockey games, went camping with them, and showered them with time that was so much more important than just intellect. I envied them, craved that kind of notice so much that I sought out anything that might fill the void. I was drawn to boys, their response to me was exhilarating, and I was quickly addicted to it.

9. Basic to man's nature is the endeavor to share, which, if successful, precludes loneliness, arrogance, and being devious; friendship is based on mutual sharing; trust is the recognition of when an individual does not threaten another by sharing; fear is the hiatus between the act of sharing and the establishment of trust; "hurt" results from rejection of one human by another with whom friendship has been established; pride for a human is the recognition of self-confidence (resulting from behavior without contradiction); sensitivity is the ability to share such pride.

Point number 9 almost reads like a map to remaining authentic—a map but not the road itself. Dad must have been extremely lonely. To the outsider looking in, he was surrounded by his boisterous family and a marriage that spread over decades. But his word choices revealed a kind of distance between him and those he loved. "Endeavor," he says. "If," he says, that friendship is based on "mutual sharing," and "trust is the recognition of when an individual does not threaten another by sharing." I have often thought that people can only give what another is willing to receive. Since matters of the heart immobilized Dad, I fear he distrusted relationships.

I remember when Dad came home from a business trip, how timorous I was in his presence. He moved at an alarming speed, in a hurry, as if he were late for a train. My mother's pace was slower. She was the constant force in a house filled with children. She was the anchor of my early childhood. Her love of poetry, literature, and stories provided the essence of who I am, and her constancy meant safety. Dad's every return into the equilibrium of my life was, for me, like the space shuttle landing in the driveway— that noise coupled with the uncertainty of what his re-entry might bring.

I can picture being carried on his shoulders and how he would shout "low bridge" when we came to a door. I can feel his hand on my lower back as he pushed me on the swing in our backyard. He would bow, arm crossed over his belly with a grin, if he had done something for me and I thanked him. His laugh was one of those knee-slapping, hushed, choking laughs that always ended in a pure coughing fit.

I remember him berating my brother for placing a piece of mail in the wrong postal box; his shout and my crying were the only sounds heard in the otherwise still car. The incident prompted me to later ask my mother why Dad didn't love my brother. She dismissed me with a hollow disclaimer. "Of course your father loves your brother."

I remember an incident on the side of a road. Somehow a suitcase had flown from the roof of the car. I can still see it, a red, dented Samsonite with scrapes from the asphalt. When we had restored it to the roof and were ready to leave, my brother was nowhere to be found. We were frantic that he wouldn't return. We found him and I was too young to understand that my father's cutting words were why he ran off, yet there he was like the red Samsonite, his dent evident in the traces of spent tears.

I recall riding his back at Memorial Drive Country Club in the pool, Dad's flesh slippery from lotion and I couldn't seem to hold on. We were underwater and his skin felt foreign to my fingers as I struggled to hold my breath. And I can still feel the softness of his crew cut beneath my touch, and hear his laugh as I slapped his outstretched hand in answer to his request for "twenty-five cents, please." He could blow a perfect smoke ring. He could fill the room on Christmas Eve with his telling of *The Night before Christmas*.

When he was displeased, the words "This is *very* discouraging" would roll off his tongue as if there were nothing worse you could do in life than to feed his disenchantment. I remember looking out the window of my bedroom on the second floor of our house in Stamford, watching him remove beer bottles from the Volvo I had crashed just a week after getting my license. He never said a word about the obvious evidence of alcohol's involvement in the wreck.

As if from a great distance I can still hear him sing, "I see you are a logger and not just a common bum / for no one but a logger stirs coffee with his thumb." I loved watching him sing, but now the song haunts my memory. "The weather, it tried to freeze him, it tried its level best / and at a hundred degrees below zero he buttoned up his vest." I can see his fingers walking up his chest, a show of buttoning in time to his song. "It froze clear down to China, it froze to the stars up above / and at a thousand degrees below zero it froze my logger love." He pointed up and down along with the song and then hugged himself. "They tried in vain to thaw him and would you believe me, sir? / They made him into axe blades to chop the Douglas fir. / And so to this café I have come / to sit and wait for someone who stirs coffee with his thumb."

To me, Dad was like a geode—beneath that rough exterior there was a splendor that was staggering, even at times inspiring. Too often, however, his beauty remained wrapped in that brittle, protective shell.

I believe I truly thought there was something beautiful, glittering beneath Derrick's brittle shell. I wanted to change him and had no understanding at that raw age that living with potential is exactly and only that. Derrick had a homing device for me; I shouldered his pain and bore the responsibility of his every misstep. I provided excuses for his behavior and understanding for his pain. Clearly my own tendency to take responsibility was in sharp contrast to Derrick's pervasive need to blame.

While growing up Derrick witnessed violence and later suffered the fallout of divorce. In my own family I was rewarded for my independence, ability to self-examine, and be accountable. I was predisposed to be help-ful—even if it meant risking my own wellbeing. The adage "Do unto others, as you wish for them to do unto you" comes to mind, and I experienced my own version: *Do unto others, even at the risk of doing yourself in.* We are all "products of our environment"—another of Dad's many axioms. How right he was.

Hi.

I finally told my parents that I was moving in with Derrick. Dad looked like I had stabbed him in the stomach or something, then he just shook his head. Ugh, I hate when he does that. I can hear him in my head, "This is very discouraging," even though he didn't say it out loud, but I could tell he was thinking it. Mom did the old hand-in-the-chin thing and looked down at her lap like she's inspecting it for something. I felt "little" there for a minute. Jeez . . .

Dad finally spoke up. "Elin, this is your life, your mother and I are not going to tell you what to do. We don't think this is a great idea but again, it's your life."

Yeah, I feel like a loser. I hate when he does that. It's like the guilt thing. It's not working on me. He did tell me I have to work full time because he can't insure me if I'm not in school. So? I was planning on that anyway. I guess I need to check out that bank. School is out in a month. He's right, it is my life and I am going to live it!

I told Derrick about their reaction and he kind of just sidestepped it by saying, what did I expect, for them to throw me a party? Whatever that means. What is with everyone?!

Hi E-Babes,

Happy Eighteenth Birthday! Finally!!!! Now I don't have to carry my stupid fake ID anymore. I had such a great birthday! We celebrated at Lou's on Saturday night (last night) and a ton of people showed up. It was so cool, almost all my friends were there. Yeah, well not Alex, that's not her gig. She's all into her new boyfriend, Ben. I get it, I really don't see Derrick and Ben hanging out anyway, but Lisa, Kelli, Jillian, Sydney . . . all kinds of people were there. It was such a blast.

My parents had a little dinner for me tonight and Derrick actually came over, it was fine, maybe a little awkward but Rod was there and that totally helped. He is always so great with people . . . making them feel comfortable. Dad even kept his cool, didn't do the whole interrogation thing to Derrick. Mom's always nice so that's not an issue ever. I think Derrick had a good time, when he left he made a nice comment about everyone so that's a start.

Thank goodness Dad didn't bring up the bit about us living together. I was kind of on the edge of my seat. Dad seemed kind of quiet. I don't think he totally likes Derrick or something. I don't know, I get the feeling that he is assessing him behind his glasses. Not that I really care! Well, maybe a little bit. Ugh! I just want school over with and move to the next phase! I am so done with living with my parents and all that . . . one more month!!!

Hey E!

I just hung up with John Hall, the manager at the bank near the apartment, and I have the job! I am so excited! Maybe a little nervous—I'm not exactly Miss Numbers—but hey, that's what the computer is for. He seems really cool, you know, not all formal and stuffy, just a good guy. I start right after graduation.

Hey E,

Well, it's official—I now have my high school diploma! The ceremony was totally boring but afterward Mom and Dad took the family out for a celebration dinner. It was really fun—we hardly ever go out to restaurants so that was a nice treat. I am done with school! Anyway, I move into Derrick's place tomorrow and start my new job on Monday. Can't wait. Look out, world, here I come!

———

Hi E,

I am all "moved in." We are super busy—work, laundry, cooking, parties— people over all the time. It's as if every day blends into the next. I have met a few people at work and so far Sue is really the only one worth hanging out with and somewhat John, too. At first Sue and I did not hit it off. She says I was a bitch. OK, first Kelli now Sue, what the heck! But now it's all cool, we have contests to see who can have the most transactions and the longest line stupid really but it makes the work day go by really fast.

I like that work is super close to my apartment, too. Sue lives on Greenwich Avenue with her friend Jane. Jane's a little quiet but oh well. We've all been going out together to places like The Depot. Derrick actually likes her, which is a nice change. I think that she is the first friend to receive any form of endorsement from him!

———

Hi E,

We had a huge barbeque here at "The Tombs," that's the nickname for the apartment we all share 'cause it's kind of dark. ("Tenebrous." OK, why do I remember stuff like this? A vocabulary word? Means: dark and gloomy . . . what a dork!) So anyway, the BBQ was so much fun. Derrick was on fire, just so funny with his job as cook . . . oh sorry, chef . . . if you can call a spatula-wielding, hot dog-roasting, hamburger-flipping guy a chef. All our good friends came over. This part was not so great—Drew brought Janet. She's nice and all but at one point she pulled me aside and asked me how it was going with Derrick. I kind of was like "What do you mean?"

"Is he nice to you?"

"Yeah, why? That's kind of a weird question."

"Elin, it's probably not my business but . . . well, you seem really nice and . . . well, I was really close to Rita."

"Yeah. I heard."

"No, nothing like that, she's glad that they aren't together."

"What do you mean?"

"Look, maybe I shouldn't say anything." We both see Drew staring at us.

"No, it's OK. Sorry, I just get super sick of everyone always bringing up Saint Rita, it kind of gets old, if you know what I mean."

"Yeah, no, I get it."

"So, Janet, what are you trying to say?"

"Maybe it's different with you guys, Elin, maybe I shouldn't . . . " Drew's still watching us and she seems a little uncomfortable.

"It's alright, really. Just tell me what you wanted to say; I want to know . . . seriously."

"Rita left him, Elin. She left him because he used to beat her up."

"What?"

"Yeah."

"Janet, I don't know what went on with them but there's no way. I mean, he gets jealous and all but nothing like that. My God, the first night we really noticed each other he laid into a guy for threatening me. I don't see it. Brett? Yeah, I would believe that, his brother's an ass, but no way Derrick . . . he would never."

Hi E,

Mom helped me sign up for the fall class at Parsons, just one class. Derrick thinks it's weird that I have to go into the city. It's the best school for that. Why does he care anyway? I mean it's one night a week. Not that big of a deal. It's still a ways off anyway. We need to get laundry done—glaciers of clothes—and bring the recycling for money.

To me,

It all happened so fast. One minute we were arguing, Logan and Sue were not home, and the next thing I knew he somehow grabbed me and threw me onto the bed in one move and then he was on me, punching me in the stomach . . . no, pummeling me. I was screaming at him, "STOP!!!! DERRICK, STOP!!! WHAT IS WRONG WITH YOU? DDDDEEEERRRRIIIICCCCKKKK SSSSSTTTTTTOOOPPPP!!!"

I was completely hysterical. I was trying to get away and defend myself and he's in my ear, "You little fucking bitch. Don't you ever tell me when to be home. I'm fucking older than you. You think you know it all, you high school graduate? I got news for you . . . you don't know shit . . . " On and on telling me how he knows, he knows what's right, not me. He knows what's right for him, for me . . . he knows . . .

He knows? What's right for me? Punches . . . are those right? Is that right for me?

It was as if my whole sense of orientation had been dislocated. I know this because the next thing I hear is my voice . . . and I am apologizing . . . I am apologizing to him . . . . to him?

"Derrick . . . Derrick, stop . . . listen . . . I'm sorry . . . stop . . . . I'm sorry I wasn't thinking" . . . . Please . . . this isn't happening . . . pretend it . . . pretend . . . Derrick, this didn't happen.

He stopped. We are both crying now and then he's holding on to me bawling. "Elin . . . oh my God . . . Elin . . . I am so sorry . . . I didn't mean to hurt you but when you told me I should have been home for dinner? I just lost it. I love you. I don't know what happened. You . . . you have to believe me. I can't live without you. Please . . . please believe me."

What was I sorry for? I actually made him dinner hours ago, even now his plate sits untouched on the table. I am sitting here alone in utter disbelief. I begged him to forgive me. I must be sorry, as in a sorry excuse for a human being. Who lets that happen? Me? Did I let that happen? I guess I did. I wanted the real world—no school, just the real world. Wasn't I just so smart? Real world just pulled up and he's driving a piece of crap truck.

I can't even think about my family . . . each one of them . . . especially my brothers . . . Dad . . . they'd literally want to kill him. That cannot happen again. He was so upset after the whole thing. It probably was over within a minute but then it was almost even worse. His grief, it's so dense, like a thick fog. I can't see him (or me) but the grief is all around us and my face is wet from crying.

———

To me,

Things are better, you know, since the last time I wrote. We had a really, really long talk about the whole thing. I put it all out there and just told him no way, can't do it. He promised me he wouldn't let it happen again. I even confronted him about Rita, and he admitted that it had been a problem. He said with her he would just lose his temper and it was like he saw "red" and he couldn't control himself. (So that's what "seeing red" means.) He told me he loves me more than anything, more than he loves himself. He said he would kill himself if anything happened to me.

"Whoa, kill yourself? Come on, that is so un-cool."

"I would, Elin, seriously, I won't live without you."

"You're scaring me . . . "

"I'm not trying to scare you, that's just how much I love you. I need you. You are the best thing that ever happened in my miserable little life. You are my life."

"Derrick, your life isn't miserable and I am not going anywhere. I just can't handle the hitting thing. It's really not OK. We have this great thing going here. We have fun, we love each other, we both have work, there's Abby . . . just the hitting. It's screwed up. My mom always said, 'Hands are for holding not hitting.' She's right, ya know? Seriously, I love you, but I can't handle that . . . at all."

"Hands are for holding, yeah, hands are for holding. Still I won't live without you, baby. You have no idea how much I love you. You're everything to me."

I am everything? Maybe we need our own place or should get out of Greenwich or something. This town sucks. Everyone is so about themselves and their money and everything. We should . . . we should just leave . . . ugh . . . or not. Like that's going to work. I love him so much I just want to take all his pain away. I can't even explain how broken he seems on the inside. How can I possibly fix that emptiness? I wonder what he feels like inside his head. When he is telling me all of this he is almost rambling. It's like listening to a guy on a street corner who is not all there. He is looking at me and smoking and all that smoke is drifting around him, but it's as if he really can't see me. He kept shaking his head like it hurt or he was disagreeing with what he was saying. I don't know. I feel that helplessness again as if it's in a bag strapped to my back.

To me,

Now what? I promised myself. God, I feel completely lost. Why? Why does he have to have such an awful temper? It was like he was Brett tonight . . . just nasty . . . mean . . . horrible.

We were just hanging out watching TV. The phone rang and Derrick answered and he says to me, "Your faggot friend Reed's on the phone." He's handing me the phone as he is saying this and not quietly. I look at him like "Shhhh!" He takes the phone back then and cups the speaker and says, "I'll kill him . . . I will," then he hands me the phone back. I was shaking.

"Hi Reed." My voice was all wobbly like I was gonna cry.

"Elin, what the hell is going on? What is his problem? Are you going to tolerate that? I'll kick his ass."

"Yeah . . . " Derrick rips the phone out of my hand and hangs it up.

And then it starts . . . the wrath.

"You littlecuntwhore . . . you and your hippy friends and that burn-out school. How the hell did they let you graduate, huh?? What, does that upset you? Yeah, try your psychobabble crap on someone who gives a shit. Get out of here. I don't even want to see your face. Go home, whore."

Now he's pushing me toward the door so I try to leave. Is that not what he wanted? Then he grabs me back, twists my arm behind my back, shoves me onto the ground, and puts his knee on my back. Then he's in my ear . . . that hideous whisper . . . "You little slut no good whore. I can't even look at your face." While he's saying that, with his other hand he grabs my hair. I am crying and trying to get him off me but he has my arm twisted behind my back and I just can't get away, and then he's pulling my hair and smashing my face into the carpet.

"LET GO OF ME, DDDDDEEERRRRIIICCCKKK, STOPPPPP!" And he stops, and so again I get up and again I hear him tell me to just leave. I try to pick up a few clothes and I'm trying to do that and out of nowhere a boot smashes me right by the temple.

I lose it. "WHAT IS WRONG WITH YOU, YOU ASSHOLE? GET AWAY FROM ME, I HATE YOU!!" *It hurt so bad. I am crying and I completely aban-don the idea of getting any of my stuff because my brain is yelling, "GET THE HELL OUT OF HERE!"*

Then I remember that my stupid car is broken. I run past it and into the parking lot and I hear him behind me. "ELIN, WAIT!" I am running and I can still hear him. "WAIT. ELIN, COME ON. PLEASE, ELIN STOP!!!!!!" I can hardly see for all the tears in my eyes and I am trying to figure out a plan in my head and . . . would he just stop yelling for me already . . . "Run," I am telling myself, "Run," but my feet start s-l-o-w-i-n-g d-o-w-n and I feel myself collapsing from the inside out and I am screaming inside to keep going, don't look back, don't . . . and then I can't take it 'cause he won't stop yelling and running behind me.

"NO!!!! NO DERRICK . . . I'M DONE. I can't . . . I CAN'T . . . you are stealing me from me . . . I can't . . . " I am sobbing.

"Fine. Take the fucking truck. Ya know what, Elin? I AM DONE. You're done? You think you're done? I say, I tell you, take my fucking truck . . . cunt."

I snap again . . . bend down to pick up the keys he just chucked at my feet and I heave them as far as I can into the bushes at the edge of the parking lot. "I DON'T WANT YOUR TRUCK. I DON'T WANT YOU." I turn around and start walking, not even fast, just deliberately, all the while wondering where am I going. I am so lost . . . displaced . . . spent. Should I go to Lisa's? Her house isn't such a long walk. All my stuff is at home . . . at the apart-ment. Home? That's not home . . . not like any home I have ever known.

My feet feel as if I have ankle weights on, every step is a work of labor and, as I cross Millbank Avenue I hear the collar. I turn around and running up the deserted street is Abby. Way behind her, he almost looks like a char-acter in a doll house, his figure is so little. I stop and Abby catches me.

"Hey Abby." As I kneel to pet her I lose it all over again. My tears are unstoppable and I hang onto her as if she is a life ring. "Abby, what am I

going to do? I hate this . . . I hate how I feel . . . I am drowning . . . Abby, help me . . . "

I could see his boots, the distance between us evaporating into thin air. I can't let go of the dog. She just let me hold her and never even flinched, that beautiful blond German shepherd. The waterline is now over my head . . . I can't breathe.

"Elin . . . hey . . . oh . . . God . . . I am so . . . sorry . . . hey, come home . . . I swear I'll get help or something . . . babe . . . come on . . . I love you . . . you know I won't live without you. You know that . . . "

You know the rest, "babe" back into the arms of the outraged. How can I be so dumb? He promised he would get help. He promised he'd stop himself. So we walk back to the Tombs and all I can think about is being on a plane and the flight attendant's message about oxygen masks. "If you are traveling with a small child, secure the oxygen mask over your own face before attaching your child's." I said it in my head a thousand times and each time the voice inside my head keeps asking me, "Who's the child, who's little?" and no answer materializes.

When we get back I crawl into bed and cry. He doesn't even touch me. He doesn't say a word, just lets me sob into my already overfilled pool of grief.

I am sitting here with this notebook, scrawling out my pitiful life. You are the only one I can tell. If he does it again, I swear I will be gone. Literally. GOING, GOING . . . G-O-N-E. Poof.

AT BIRTH MY mother named me Wendy, Wendy Bell. My grandma said my name was like a boat—"The Wendy Bell." It seemed that everywhere my mother went, she heard "Wendy!" as other mothers called their own daughters back to them from underneath clothes racks or down grocery store aisles, and the sinking feeling that she had given me the wrong name took hold. When I reached the ripe age of nine months she took me to court and once the judge confirmed with a chuckle that I had not committed any crimes, he granted me, in my mother's arms, my new name.

My brother Rod said I was confused by all this. He remembers coming down the stairs that opened into our kitchen and seeing me in my high chair. "Hi Elin!" he called. Nothing. "Elin?" Nothing. With a glance over the shoulder to make sure our mother wasn't on his heels, he whispered, "Wendy!" I responded with a jerk of the head, eye contact, and a smile.

Wendy was easy to pronounce, no one had to spell it, and by the time I was ten I sort of wanted it back. Ironically, this was seven years before Elin Nordegren would be born and a full thirty-six years until her marriage to Tiger Woods would let the world know that the name Elin has a long E.

Mom told me that *Pat the Bunny* was my favorite book. The hard-page book had whiskers to feel, flowers to smell, and a bunny to pet. When we reached the end with the little foil mirror my mother would point and say, "Look, there's Elin!" to which I would definitively shake my head and say, "No! Winny!" And there it was, our first disagreement. She saw Elin and I saw Wendy.

Is that how it begins? As parents do we see our children only through our own lens? When I was with Derrick, I surreptitiously tiptoed past my parents' field of vision. They saw me as capable, strong, and independent. That was how I wanted them to see me. Like the baby shaking her head, I could not begin to explain to them what was happening to me. I did not understand that I was a victim of dating violence and had lost control of my life. I was humiliated and frightened but truly I believed I would be able to fix it.

My parents had no idea about the red flags of abuse in a relationship; in those days domestic abuse of any kind was largely kept behind closed doors. There were no lists of what to look for made available to parents whose neck hairs were standing on end. They knew something was off, but violence would have been the last thing they would have suspected. With utter stealth I managed to cover myself in long garments that hid the cuts and bruises—a subtle yet definitive sign. I told myself it would all be all right. And my parents did not detect that I was crumbling inside nor did they see that he was cutting me off from them—isolation, another red flag. My increasing inability to be alone was shaped by a madman who convinced me that making decisions was not my forte.

To me,

There are days where Derrick will get a side job with Drew, you know, make some money. Those are the good days. On those days I can see him, I watch from the window inside. I see him pull out of the parking lot in that truck, behind the windshield, with his head craned to see what's behind him, and once securely from the slot that is the truck's home, he turns back forward and seems to look in my direction. Does he see me? Does he see me? I watch as if my life is lying in the balance of the very answer I am looking for. No, I think, he doesn't. The cigarette dangles from his lips and the glow is visible; without the benefit of seeing into the cab I can picture his paw-like hand shifting the truck into first, foot on the clutch, and slowly he pulls away.

On these days that are good, I shower with purpose and get ready for work. I tell Abby that she is the best dog in the entire world and whisper quietly that she is my lifesaver. She loves me, she sees me, this wonderful, sweet dog. I take my leave and head to the bank where my world transforms into something apart from The Tombs. I am free to laugh, to play, to be silly . . . even to flirt. I like my work because I like the people. This boring-to-look-at red-brick building with a safe the size of our apartment feels a little more like home every day.

On those good days, we almost always go down to The Depot or over to The Grill and have drinks and pizza. On those days he laughs with me and tells me he loves me and I pray to a God I don't believe in to give me another day just like today. Those are the good days.

———

To me,

So I started that class in NYC a month and a half ago and it's OK, a little bit of a hassle because I have to get off work, get to the train station, park, and get my ticket all within twenty-two minutes. Once I'm on the train, well, that part's great. The rumbling of the train beneath my feet rocks me into a different time; tonight I was back in Europe, I bicycled all over Scotland, England, and France with the Student Hostelling Program, two years ago. It feels like ten. Man, was that an amazing trip! I can almost smell the farms in Scotland through my shut eyes. I was so hung up on Fergus at that point in my life that I could hardly focus on the beauty that surrounded me. Now I would give anything to be there. Alone.

Fergus . . . I look out the window and watch the towns disappear . . . Port Chester, Rye, Harrison. My breath fogs the window and I trace a tiny heart, then erase it. The chill on the glass reminds my touch winter is around the bend . . . Mamaroneck, Larchmont. The conductor's announcements are comforting like a familiar lullaby from childhood . . . New Rochelle, Pelham . . . My mom is from Pelham . . .

The city is a welcome diversion from Greenwich. I have spent a tremendous amount of time rummaging through Greenwich Village and SoHo. Lorna and Paul both live here and yet I hardly think of them navigating the streets when I am here. I still sort of see all of us at our old water's-edge house . . . but they are here in NY.

Arriving in Grand Central always makes me feel good. There's the familiar release of the train brakes, which makes a loud PSSSST, and for a brief second it's almost like being in a movie, disembarking into the very guts of the city. It always feels sort of warm and the smell permeates my being, that concrete, somewhat dirty, dank New York odor that for some reason always makes me almost wish I lived here. I never tire of Grand Central, the amazing ceiling. If only I could defy gravity and float among her star-speckled ceiling. No, I am down here on the ground but I always crane my neck as I wind my way to the Lexington Avenue subway and the familiar journey to my Union Square classroom one night a week.

Fashion. Ironic really. I have zero desire to pursue anything remotely connected to the fashion industry. Maybe I am living my mother's fantasy. I'm actually good at it or could be if I worked at it. But I won't. Each time I leave I wonder whether I will ever come back, and each week that I arrive back on this quasi-movie set I am almost baffled that I am here.

By the time I get home I am always (no exception) exhausted. Tonight is no different. What is different is that I can hear the partiers as soon as I open the car door. Ugh, not tonight, I have to work tomorrow. I would put all the money I have on a bet in Vegas that Derrick did not make it to the laundromat. I feel the fatigue set in my jaw. Wipe it away . . . wipe it away . . . deep breath . . . man, they're loud . . . who all is in there?

I open the door and there in front of me is an old friend of Derrick's who we haven't seen in ages. It's been—I don't know—six months? He is quite obviously buzzed and in his enthusiasm leaps toward me and picks me up off the floor in a bear hug. I didn't even see it coming. Abby launches herself from wherever she was when I walk in the door to his crotch, all teeth. Thank goodness for our buddy he has on really baggy cords; she tore right through the fabric and he just about fell over from surprise.

"ABBY!" I hear Derrick yell.

"Sam, oh my God, I am so sorry!!!" I say as I grab Abby. She is not sure if she did the right thing or not.

"Man, Derrick, nice dog. Jeez, Elin, I guess she loves you!" He's laughing now, and I am petting Abby and get down and hug her and in her ear I say,

"I know, girl, you're my savior." She licks me and bolts from the room. I wish I could follow her to her corner bed and curl up into a world where I had no job the next day or laundry to do or recycling to take in for nickels so we can buy more beer and eat.

I look at Derrick for confirmation that this really is a good day and he smiles (that smile that melts everything away) and I reach for his embrace and hear him whisper, "Hey, beautiful, welcome home, I sure love you, ya know." I can smell the beer but turn my disapproval inward and reach for my own to join him in his good day.

MAX AND I camped just days ago 200 feet above the Pacific Ocean atop a sand dune. When we woke, a fog hugged the coast. The beach was barely visible way below.

"Let's go!" Max said, and minutes later we were making our way down. He treated the forty-degree-angled trail like a sand ski run. I, on the other hand, slithered while thinking about the undeniable fact that I would have to climb back up later.

We walked and talked alongside the roaring ocean, sharing the comfort of each other's company. Soon the four-mile hike back to the car loomed before us, and we both gazed at the seemingly insurmountable hill above.

"Imagine carrying a ninety-pound German shepherd up this trail in ninety-degree weather, Mom," he said through a grin, knowing that this image would spur me on in the bad moments ahead. I had heard the story more than once: His friend's dog wouldn't go up the hill so Max hoisted him and carried him to the top. Today he continued his instruction: "For every three steps you take, it will be like one because you *will* slip backward. It's OK, though—just maintain your balance and keep going."

"You go first," I said. "I don't want to hold you back." His immediate ascent was his agreement, and I watched him take the hill, wondering when he became so capable.

The entire way up I kept saying to myself, "I am not the dog. I am not the dog." Twice I needed to empty my sneakers of sand, but miraculously I did make it to the top.

"I am NOT the dog!" I announced as I arrived at our campsite.

He beamed at me. "You would kick the butts of 90 percent of the kids I went on that geology trip with, Mom, and that was tough!" I was somewhat surprised by how incredibly satisfying that comment was to my aging ego.

My dad had the same ability to feed my self-esteem. He would say things like, "Isn't that just nifty!" or "By God, Elin, you tell them!" and make me feel as if I could do anything. Lately, the grief I feel for him is unpredictable; it pops up like something stowed in the pocket of a jacket not worn often. You feel it, pull it out, and whatever memory it invokes is suddenly all around you like sunlight breaking through a cloud. That was my dad. He was the sun that is all around me right now because his enthusiasm and faith still buoy me.

In sharp contrast, there is my mom. She is not one to ooze or bellow compliments like a band instrument. Now that he is gone, her demeanor feels guarded, quiet, even remote.

After she read the first draft of my book all the way through, her main comment was "I am just heartbroken for that poor dog, left to die alone like that."

The dog? I thought. *This memoir is not about a dog, this memoir is about your daughter.* But my cowardly answer was, "I know, it is heartbreaking, isn't it."

But nearly a year later I still feel gutted.

Years after my relationship with Derrick was over I learned Abby had died. He went on a bender and forgot her and she starved to death.

In many ways, Abby and I are the same. The dog and I were both victims of human abuse. I was starved for validation, not food, and I fed that starvation with whatever love was the loudest. Derrick begged me to stay and maintained he couldn't live without me. His needs left no room for my own. He threatened to kill himself, me, my family, and the dog—and I believed him. The fear I felt paralyzed and silenced me.

The dog could not call out for help and neither could I, and in that silence we both died.

My thoughts turn to my own children. The idea of any one of them suffering an abusive relationship unhinges me. I know it can happen. My own parents missed it. Like the dog, I did not have the power, I did not have the voice . . . he had it . . . and I could not call out.

And I know now that I was no different from any teen who endures an abusive relationship. As in a drowning, the abuse victim is pulled under, and unless the parent is standing right at the water's edge paying attention, the lack of oxygen wins.

My family rarely saw me, and when they did I was often in a hurry to leave. Sign number one. I withdrew—my friends did not hear from me. Sign number two. I wore long sleeves and long pants—all the time. Sign number three. I was very thin—not eating. Sign number four. I had a distinct inability to make a decision. Sign number five. I never, ever drove—he always did. Sign number six. I was working two jobs—he did nothing. Sign number seven.

Signs—they were there but under the surface and not really visible unless you were standing next to the pool. As a mother I am abundantly aware that I must always keep my eye on the waterline.

I am not the dog . . . I am not the dog . . . I am *not* the dog.

To Whom It May Concern:
It's only happened more frequently. Months ago I had this overwhelming desire to believe it would stop. I thought he wanted to change. I believed him.

We argue more than not now. It doesn't always turn into a war zone but there again, we are not always alone in the apartment. The Tombs—how fitting. I know he doesn't mean to hurt me. He sees "red" and any sense of control is lost into a whirlwind of what seems to me hours of chaos and fear. It's as if I am living in Kansas, alone, no underground shelter and over the radio I hear a tornado warning. I remain in my house waiting . . . wondering. Will it come? Will it happen? Or will it just be a strong wind? Violence is like weather; without radar it is unpredictable. I am awake now. I am awake.

Tornado Warning

Last night I dreamt
I lived alone
on a farm
Kansas . . .
oh, so vast
Tornado Warning
blared through a radio
oh, so clear
and there
on the porch
I watched a soldier
The King of Hearts
(didn't he save the crazy ones?)
and waited
as the sky
poured colors of
cold grey
Across the horizon
the wind paused
to pick up
yesterday's news . . .
"Earth is older and in control"
No Hope
I felt my body

Being
sucked into the
spinning cone
my dreams, ambitions, hopes
and fears
gathered in the arms
of a whirling maniac
never to be released . . .
last night
I dreamt, I lived
Alone

———

To Whom It May Concern:

I can't keep it in anymore. How am I supposed to go on trying to convince myself that he will change or that somehow this is the new normal . . . it can't be. My dad never did this to my mother.

Why me? Am I so unworthy of something good? Something special? Is it written in destiny that this is my future? How can anyone look me in the eye and tell me there is a God in heaven who cares? I allow it so I deserve it. All that I give . . . the only thing he has given me is black and blue.

Love me, somebody, please. Who am I?

People always say walk a mile in my shoes. How the hell did I get these shoes on my feet? Look at them, these shoes I am wearing. They don't fit, I don't even like them. I just need to get them off my feet then throw them away. Burn them at the stake. Shoot them full of holes. Drown them in the harbor. Bury them in the yard. Anything so that no one has to wear them again, ever. There is no salvation army for these shoes.

I sometimes look at those little fine tight curls at the base of his hairline and I just want to pull them out one by one, then move my hand to his neck and strangle him until I see his last breath escape his blue lips. I must be ccccccrrrraaaaazzzzyyyy, certifiably insane.

What was I ever attracted to? I think back to that first night . . . he was so . . . heroic . . . saved by a fucking maniac . . . nice . . . no, but he smiled at me and he made me feel safe . . . he seemed so human. I wonder if the guy who wrote Dr. Jekyll and Mr. Hyde *beat his wife?*

I have only loved him. I have poured all of me into him and now I am nowhere to be seen. He broke my spirit. My eyes are full of water. My heart aches. I hate who I have become. I want to go back. I want to be sixteen.

I can't remember what it's like to laugh. He absconded with my very soul. How did he take it?

I try so hard to believe that none of this will happen again. Is it a game for him? Am I a pawn? His anger is killing me. He wants to marry me . . . what? Marry you? Have your kids? Kids? So what, so you can beat all of us?

Every time you as much as put a finger on me, I flinch; everything in me clenches . . . don't you know how much I hate you for what you are doing to me??? I hate me . . . I have to get away, somehow . . .

I want myself back. I don't know this person I am trapped inside. God I wish he would change, please help me, I can't live like this.

ON OUR RETURN home from our run today, we found that it was a green-light day—all the lights ready for us as we approached each intersection. I didn't need to stop my running watch, and Chinook was spared the jerking of her leash. No need to stop time today.

Some things in life are so magical that I wish I could stop time and look at something in every detail. I wish I could revisit those moments when my kids were babies and touch them again, smell their sweet baby breath, feel their little fingers wrapped around my own, tickle a smile across their toothless faces, and hear their first words echo through the room.

Conversely, there are times I wish I could fast forward, not see, not remember, not experience, but I must face and own those unpleasant times as well. A pervasive need for rescue permeated my youth. I played on both sides of the river—the need to rescue and the need to be rescued. That tug-of-war landed me in the middle of raging waters, and I nearly drowned. I see that young girl who is me much the same way I see my own remembered babies. I want to shout through time to yell to her that if for a minute she would just look up in her frantic state she would see that she had enough air to get to the surface and that she was strong enough to make it to dry land.

I want to tell her she's worth saving, worth fighting for.

How did I get to that desperate point back then? How do we get anywhere? As Confucius said, "A journey of a thousand miles begins with a single step." Perhaps the journey is truly an infinite number of miles and we are all pioneers. My desire to mend Derrick usurped my ability to rescue myself early on, and his tragic life caught hold of me. No matter how hard I swam his furious yet tortured body clung to me as if his existence depended upon my every stroke.

Person of Concern,
Now I am a liar.

Do you think Rod believed me when I told him I fell down and that's why my arms are covered with bruises? He didn't question me. Why would he? I have never lied to him or anyone in my family. He looked so concerned and I wanted to tell him but I just couldn't. (If I tell anyone, especially my brothers, they will only want to kill Derrick.) He would only want me to understand that this isn't right . . . but I know that . . . I know it's not right. When will I feel what I understand? Rod and I had dinner together and it was great just to be alone with someone who sees me. He sees me, he really can see me.

Person of Concern,

And now it's me with the temper. If there's one thing I can't deal with it's when someone puts down a member of my family. He made some stupid-ass remark about my parents and my brother and I lost it. He doesn't have a clue!

I snapped. I slapped him across the face as hard as I could and then yelled till my throat was sore. He, not able to deal with my rampage, attempted to control me. I shook from his grasp and yelled, "Don't you ever speak about my family again." I ran out the door and slammed it in his face.

Outside I crouched down on the porch and started crying, shaking uncontrollably. I heard the unmistakable creak of the door opening and the scuff of his feet. Then I felt his arms around me from behind and he put his lips to my ear and whispered, "You're acting like me . . . "

I cried noiselessly. Of all the people in the world I would choose not to be like, you are it, I said silently, as I stood up and walked from his near embrace.

Back into the apartment, I crawled into bed with a man who doesn't have a clue who I am, nor I him. He sends shivers down my spine. I guess God won't help me . . . can I?

Derrick,

I want you to know that I'm here at the kitchen table listening as you pull in and exhale air. Like an infant you sleep. I wonder if you are tame in your dreams. Does your mind haunt you with the slow-moving frames we shot tonight? I close my eyes and see nothing.

I put my hand on my heart only to feel its steady throb. And I ask myself how much longer will this heart beat? What will it take to wake me up from this living nightmare?

I have no one I can tell this to. Shame and guilt are on me like an old army coat. Are there other people out there like me?

You, you just go on breathing. Just like there is not a problem anywhere.

You tell me I am the crazy one . . . crazy to stay? Either I am incredibly strong or pathetically weak.

It scares me. What will you do if I leave?

You told me tonight you'd kill me and yourself.

Dear Person,

Logan pulled the plug—Derrick and I are moving. Logan spoke to me privately and told me he is fed up with Derrick. I get it, he just sits home all day watching TV and smoking while I'm at work. He can't manage his part of the rent and Logan is sick inside for what he has seen me turn into.

"Elin, you are wasting away . . . what the hell do you weigh anyway?"

"What? I don't know . . . "

"Look, you are awesome, I care about you, I just can't deal with the whole Derrick show. He owes me tons of money that I know I'll never see."

"How much? I'll pay you back."

"No, Elin. That's not why I am telling you this . . . seriously it's more than the money . . . I am so sorry."

"No, I get it. OK. Seriously Logan, thanks . . . I get it."

So that was that. We couldn't find a place together so now I am at home with my folks. Derrick is up at Jake and Carter Northrop's place in Stamford. He's sleeping on the porch until a room in the main house opens up.

Derrick,

It's 11:00 p.m., well, a little after. Being back at my parent's house is still feeling a bit strange. I know I will never give you this letter but for tonight I'll pretend that you'd have enough sensitivity to understand my thoughts.

I miss living together. It sucks coming home. I feel like a failure. I hate not waking up to you, and for some reason I keep wondering if we will ever live together again. I just wrote that and I actually had to stop and re-read what I wrote. What is wrong with me? I seriously question my ability to reason with any logic whatsoever. Why do I miss you?

I feel empty, lost, and constantly panicked. Panicked that you'll find some-one else, panicked by how insecure I am (why am I so insecure?), panicked that I actually still want you, panicked by your hold on me. Why do I care? What is wrong with me? I remember all of those torturous nights and yet still I long to be with you. I have been praying (and you know that's not re-ally what I do) but I did and will. I pray that you will never hit me again.

I tell myself maybe the separation will help us. Maybe things will get better because now you are working again. I am always so tired. Why do I feel like I can never really sleep? I sleep but it's almost like I sleep with my eyes open.

I wonder what you are doing right this second. Watching TV, sleeping with the TV on, smoking, petting the dog, or maybe you are missing me. Really I don't much feel like writing. What I would really like is to talk, you know, like, an honest conversation where we share what we feel. Not going to happen.

Talk . . . that would be a miracle. Sometimes I wonder why I bother. What is life really worth to me? What the hell is so important here on earth? What have I really contributed to this world? Where would I be if I had gone to college? Or who would I be if my parents had never moved from Texas?

But here I am, spinning around in this town like a top. Wishing that you would just be nice. So, I guess I was right, I won't send this letter. Why would you read it when I can hardly even read it myself?

Hi,

Derrick called; it looks as if we are going to get a room . . . thank goodness. Living at home has been OK, but I feel split in two. Always spending my time over at Derrick's but not officially living there. It looks like we can move in next week. I told my parents that I would be moving again and they both were super quiet. There's this feeling I get from them like I have been a subject of conversation for them. Not such a great realization. I imagine I am a huge disappointment, not in college and all that. Oh well, I have to show them I can make it on my own.

I ARRIVE AT the beach for my run still feeling guilty about leaving Chinook at home. The weight of her perceived sorrow is one step behind me; she is a dog so she will get over it. In fact she may be happily sleeping this very moment.

If only forgetting were that easy. New questions skip through my bloodstream like a pebble on still water. Do we really "get over" wrongs that have been done to us? How do we know we are "healed"? The diameter of the rings created by the stone grows wider in my blood lake. I can almost see the ripple appear beneath my skin. Maybe "healed" isn't the objective. What if it is "healing"—as in ongoing, like the ocean in a constant ebb and flow? The rolling of the waves begins to settle over me, giving way to a more lucid view of the past that has shaped me. It is as if introspection serves as a ceremonial ablution and through that ritual the chokehold of shame is rinsed clean and makes room for me to see that I am not a victim. I am a survivor, but there's more. I need to thrive, share, prevent. I can no longer stay quiet in this world, I have a voice and I feel it reverberate off my internal walls, making its slow climb upward until its melody can be heard all around.

The water is so clear today. The scattered surfers are protected by their full-length wet suits. I so admire the surfers out there in the frigid waters bobbing up and down, void of fear. I can swim in my mind, backstroke to a time when each of my children played on this beach, their fortitude and very being providing me with inspiration. I am suddenly overwhelmed with gratitude. It is a privilege to be a parent, having a hand in the miracle of bearing and raising children.

Yet this miracle also brings responsibility. As parents, what can we do to prepare our children for the cruelty that exists? We zip our children into a proverbial full-body wet suit lined with life's eruditions, a neoprene triple-layer fabric of wisdom to ward off hypothermia, scrapes, and snares. We smear UV70 sunblock across their faces, hands, and feet as if our mere touch and each application will prevent the ruthless incursion of any future cancer.

I can no more imagine one of my children experiencing violence than I can orbit the moon. I hear myself thinking things such as, "Over my dead body," or "I'd kill the person who lays a finger on any one of them." But all that bravado gives way to an utterance, a borderline beseeching that re-states how I can handle it: Send the tough stuff to me . . . please keep them safe . . . let them be strong from all that they do, not what they endure.

Protect, safeguard, shelter, save, harbor—yet in the long run protection is not enough. We can't just keep our children in a bubble. We need to build their strengths, sharpen their tools, let them own their triumphs as well as their mistakes. We need to help them understand the gravity of their words and actions before they hurt another person. We need to raise them to be good people, strong people, contributing people, and all that potential is predicated upon their own self-confidence. For in due course, we must open our hands in a wave, catch our breath as these independent creatures slip into the world's water. We find ourselves praying silently that this child of ours has what it takes to navigate safely.

The fog that was previously south has lifted without my noticing and now I can see clear to Mexico. I turn and gaze north. If I were a bird I could fly the coastline all the way to Santa Barbara where Max lives, or east to where Kodiak and Chandler are at their respective schools. I turn to leave the shore with the word "confidence" dissolving on my tongue as if it were a candy lifesaver.

Hey!

Things have been going great! This house situation is WAY better. We have been getting along so well and everyone who lives here is super cool. We also have excellent neighbors. We've had a few parties with those guys and pretty much everything is just fun all the time.

Work is great, too. I got a raise and a good review from John, who asked me to think about taking more responsibility like head teller. That was a surprise. He says he thinks I have good leadership skills. That made me feel really good. So we'll see!

Hey,

We had a blast last night, a whole bunch of us went sledding up at the golf course and it was really cold and so much fun! All but one of us would take the sleds and toboggans down the hill and then one person would drive Derrick's truck down and pick us all up. We were all laughing so hard and the stars were amazing, really beautiful. It felt so good to just laugh and play. Later when Derrick and I got home and all warm again we talked about how we really should do more stuff like that. Get with friends and do something instead of go to Lou's! I am all for it.

Hi,

Well, it wasn't major but we had an argument. Derrick has been leaving later for work and I told him I was worried, did he have enough work, should he be trying to get more. He got all pissed because he thinks I am trying to tell him what to do. Finally I just said, forget it, you obviously have it under control, I'll get off your back! That was it. Not a huge deal but I just get so bugged when he can't just hear what I am saying without getting all pissy!

Hey,

I saw my parents tonight and we talked a little bit about school. Mom told me about an art class she saw advertised through Fairfield University called "The Magic of Marker." It actually sounds pretty interesting, I may check it out. Dad told me he was really hoping I would consider a full-time college. He thinks it's too late for fall entrance but told me we could gather info and look at maybe January. It's nice that they are trying, I just really don't know what I would go for. I told him I was a little worried that I didn't know what I wanted to "be." My mom jumped in and said that it didn't matter right now, that just getting an education would be important. I have no idea!!!

I mentioned to Derrick about the art class and he just said something like, "Whatever floats your boat," code for "That sounds stupid." At least we didn't get in a fight about it.

To me,

We went to Lou's after work tonight and what a screwed up night. I am sitting there with a bunch of guys, all Derrick's friends, and they are talking about motorcycles. Derrick is telling the stupid story about his old BMW bike that he had and how he loved to take his hands off the handlebars and put them on Rita's legs and people always remember seeing them around town doing that. Who cares? Shit, I just wanted to be somewhere else. So I am there but no one cared, and in walks Hunter. Great. I think to myself of all the people, now I am going to also hear about why Derrick thinks Hunter is an idiot 'cause he claims Hunter was responsible for one of his billion and two crashes on his motorcycle. Yeah, whatever, the story goes that Hunter was sitting in the middle of the road on his dirt bike talking to someone (probably David) and Derrick comes hauling ass around the corner, has to swerve to avoid hitting Hunter, and bangs up his bike a little because he drove off the road. Not a crash, just a bump.

At first Hunter didn't see me and, honestly, I almost hoped he wouldn't, but then I was feeling left out and completely over hearing about Rita, too. I watched as he ordered his beer and when he turned to get a table, he turned away from us not toward us. Just as he plopped down in his seat and started to peel his jacket off, he noticed me staring at him. I could see the smile spread across his face as our eyes met. Man, he's cute. He motions to me to join him and I turn back to the group, and they are all still completely wrapped up in their motorcycle stories so, I think to myself, what the hell.

I picked up my beer and slinked over to his table.

"Elin, Elin, Elin . . . we meet again. I see you're with your posse tonight."

"Hey Hunter, what's up? Yeah, some posse, bunch of drunks swapping lies."

"How are you, girl?"

It hits me how incredibly familiar he is to me and I somehow miss him almost to the point of tears. We all used to have so much fun together.

"Remember how we used to all go to the cabin off Cognewaugh?"

"Hell yeah, girl, you think I'd forget those days? Man, we had some fun, huh?"

"Yeah, we sure did. You seen Lisa or any of them lately?"

"Nah, everyone's off at school. How 'bout you, you always seemed like a smart person, why aren't you at school?"

"Looks are deceiving."

"Now don't go sounding like that, you sure are. Man, could you sing. You still singing?"

"Nope."

"Why the hell not?"

"I don't know . . . I really don't know, Hunter. Guess I don't feel much like it these days."

I could feel him approach before he said anything and the change in Hunter's expression only confirmed it.

"Elin, it's time to get going."

"Hey, Derrick, how's that BMW of yours?" I know he's egging him on; everyone knows the bike is gone.

"Hunter." I turn to see the hostility dance across his green eyes. In a split second I hear myself and I can't believe it.

"Derrick, I'm not ready to go, I haven't seen Hunter here in a while. Give me ten minutes or so would you?" He then shifted his focus to me and I could see he was stunned.

"Yeah, sure, I'll grab another beer." And he turned toward the bar.

"That frickin' guy hates my ass," Hunter says into his glass.

"Hey, at least it's a cute ass." I flirt with him and his eyes all at once light up again. The blue in contrast to Derrick's feels like water I could dive in to.

"I don't think your boyfriend would appreciate your assessment of my . . . ass."

"Yeah, well he's over there and he doesn't know half of our history, let alone all of it."

I watch him think about that.

"Yup, that was some history, got both our 'asses' in trouble, now didn't it?" He chuckles as if he's made a joke and I think about David. It feels like a lifetime ago. I suddenly feel old, ancient, tired. I change the subject and listen to how Hunter is living at home and working, same old crap with his parents but a little better than high school. He doesn't really get out much—no girlfriend, Sophia broke his heart. I hear him but I feel myself getting jumpy, like a deer who detects a lion, it knows danger is near and it runs. Unlike the deer, I don't have the brains to run.

"Elin, let's go." I turn, this time his jacket's on and he's holding mine.

"Good to see ya, Hunter."

"You, too, Elin, you take good care of yourself." His eyes drift up to Derrick's. "Derrick."

"Hunter." They nod at each other almost like two old guys from New Hampshire would, their general discord for one another not giving way to social pleasantries. As soon as I am up, Derrick grabs my arm by the triceps as if he were grabbing onto a pull-up bar with one hand. It's not friendly, and I can feel my heart race. I know he's pissed. With his free hand he punches the door open and all but forces me to the car. Given it's spring, it's really cold out and the chill brings on shivering that I can't control.

"WHAT THE FUCK WAS THAT ALL ABOUT?"

"What are you talking about?"

"WHAT AM I TALKING ABOUT?? ARE YOU FUCKING KIDDING ME?!" He punched the steering wheel and I jumped a little and as I did I moved closer to my door. Didn't we just drive here with me practically in his lap I was sitting so close to him with his hand on my leg? The heat is blasting and he reverses the car. Oh, this will be a fun drive home. He drove like a bat out of hell the entire way up Valley Road, onto Palmer Hill, then Still Water. By the time we finally navigated onto Cold Spring Road I could almost see the anger evaporate . . . not sure if it was the alcohol, the drive, any of it; it could have been a thousand things. My hand was still gripped onto the door as if I might spring from the moving car. I was crying (of course) but quietly. Kind of like when I'm afraid to draw attention to myself, you know, facing the window and not wiping the tears or sniffling. As I stared out the window and watched Cos Cob turn into Riverside and Riverside into Stamford I couldn't stop thinking about Hunter. Derrick didn't say a word after his brief outburst and striking of the steering wheel. We pulled into the driveway and the house was dark. Please be home . . . someone, please be home. I started to open the door and Derrick broke the silence.

"Look, hang on a minute . . . "

"What?" I said with a whisper, still hoping to melt into the frame of the car.

"I just can't handle it. I saw you with him and I just couldn't handle it. Shit, Elin, I can't even explain it . . . it was like you were being taken from me in front of me."

"Derrick, he's my friend, we were in school together, for God's sake, I went out with his best friend. It's not like he's an old boyfriend. I mean, really, I never see any of my friends!" Now I am sobbing . . . Ugh!

"Look, baby, I can't lose you, especially to that prick. You know I can't stand him, the cocksucker almost killed me, Elin, do you get that?"

"I wasn't there. You've told me, I know, he was in the way. My God, Derrick, do you think he planned it or something? That's just Hunter . . . the guy just does stuff like that. If you knew him, you'd know. He's a good guy...and PS, he has no interest in me, OK? He's still hung up on Sophia, for crying out loud . . . not me. He thinks of me as a buddy, almost like a sister . . . but not—" Oh man, do I need to shut up. Where am I going with this?

"Alright. alright, already . . . I just can't handle the thought of not having

you, I'd just lose it. I can't explain it. You are my everything and it just felt like a . . . I don't know...like I could just picture it, maybe not just Hunter but anyone . . . like someday you're just gonna be gone . . . someone's gonna take you from me or something."

"I'm not going anywhere. I love you . . . remember . . . I love you." We got out of the car and I almost feel like I am going to collapse from the exhaustion. When we walked through the door I could hear Carter in the kitchen. Oh thank goodness, I thought, we aren't alone.

"Derrick, I'm beat. I'm gonna go straight up to bed, OK?"

"I'm gonna grab a beer." Soundlessly I head up the stairs and I can feel my hands trembling. Everything had been so good. He held it together this time but I can see he is like a blister readying itself to pop. He can picture me leaving? Being taken? As I pull off my jewelry and place it on my bureau, I draw a line in the dust. It's a road, I tell myself. Moving an object, I create a curve, and with pure precision add an exit to my dust path. "There," I whisper to the empty room. "I need an exit." With the back of my fist I erase my handiwork and peel the layers of clothing off and step into pajamas. The stillness that surrounds me in bed serves as an added blanket of warmth and in the dark I wonder how I can really get off the road I am on.

GIVEN THAT THREE years later Hunter and I would be married, I wonder now if Derrick saw something neither Hunter nor I did. Was it there on the table at Lou's—an invisible Ouija board pulling our futures together?

Elin who?

Who am I? Where am I? Alone, I wonder, am I even awake? This feels like a fucking nightmare. Your company . . . I longed for your company. When you actually showed up you ripped my book from my hands and told me I read too much. So now the threat is a book?

"Miracles," *you snickered.* "Do you *believe in miracles?*"

"What?"

"The book . . . it's called Miracles. *Do you believe in miracles?*"

"No, not anymore, but that's not really what it's about. It's about . . . "

"I don't give a shit what it's about!" *He grabs the book and throws it across the room.*

"Why did you do that?"

"I am sick *of you reading your stupid books.*"

Hey,

We can't even buy a break. Derrick and I went up to Mike's house last night and we were all hanging out and I guess Derrick had a few too many drinks. Shocking, I know. We had all decided we'd head down to Howland's, so we're in the driveway and Derrick is checking out Mike's new BMW motorcycle. Next thing I know he's pushing Mike, almost like he's playing, and saying, "Hey, rich boy, how about you let me take Elin on the bike . . . huh?" *Another little push.*

"Naw, Derrick, tell you what, another time, OK?"

"What, you afraid I might scratch it? Huh, think I might wreck it? Is that it?" *Now he's pushing him harder and out of nowhere he takes a swing at Mike. Mistake! Mike basically takes him out. I am not even sure how it happened but Derrick can't walk. His knee is swollen to twice its size.*

Wonderful. After a really stupid argument with Mike, Derrick finally agrees to get in the car and go home with me.

So today I bring him to the doctor, and guess what? He needs surgery. Great. It's an eight-week recovery or some BS thing like that. He has to work the details out with his dad. We left with crutches and his knee wrapped. He can actually walk without the crutches, but they are for when it really hurts. The surgery should happen in three to four weeks, depending on how it gets paid for. Derrick's freaked to talk to his dad so he's in a really great mood.

Hi,

That went over like a lead balloon but there's really no choice, he has to have the surgery. His dad can be such a jerk, everything is about money. It's frickin' pathetic. He was super bent about how Derrick never gets work that pays benefits. (Yeah, I get that, my dad would be pissed, too.) But then he just berates him for his lifestyle and makes him feel like a full loser. It was horrible.

Hi,

I found a second job working at The Boat House Restaurant and Bar right near our house. Mostly I will be cocktailing but a couple of nights I'll be in the dining room. The manager said he can start me tomorrow, thank goodness. We are so broke and I am not asking my dad for money right now. I have never served drinks so I am psyched up about that. Derrick is glad that it's just up the street and actually, so am I.

To Whom It May Concern:
Are you still out there? Remember me?

Hyde is back, only he's on crutches. I cannot wait till he goes in for surgery next week. This whole thing has taken forever! I am busting my ass working two jobs. I have zero time to do anything, and because of his knee, Derrick is basically in the house watching TV all day. He can walk without crutches but not super well.

I leave our house at eight in the morning so I can be at work by 8:45. I work until 3:30 so I can be at my next job at 4:30. John at the bank has been super cool. He lets me count down my drawer early so I can leave right at 3:30. The bank closes at 3:00 so it's not that big of a deal but still, most people don't count their drawer until 3:15.

All the people at The Boat House so far are super nice. The cook, Thelma, is a crack up—kind of a Ruth Gordon type—and Summer, the bartender, is way cool, too. There are others but they are my favorites. The company policy is no boyfriends in the bar. For once, something is working in my favor. I cannot imagine Derrick sitting there while guys try to hit on me all night. He'd be turning his crutches into weapons. Yeah, he needs to never go there. Man, guys are letches, I mean in one way the attention is kind of nice but sometimes it's a little bit more than I want.

Everyone at the bank has been all over my case about my weight, so I finally weighed myself and I'm 103 pounds. OK, I guess I get it. Nothing fits but I have been so busy I just don't really think about it. My life absolutely sucks!

Then when I am home I wait on Derrick hand and foot. And have laundry to do and chores around the house. It just doesn't end.

On top of all that, he can't understand why I am not in the mood to have sex! Are you kidding me? He got super pissed because I wouldn't "get him off." Yeah, he basically fucking forced me to give him a blow job, and I was so tired, I just finally gave up on him and then he actually grabbed me by the hair and shoved my face into the goddamned bed and then hit me on the back. Somehow he twisted my arm up behind my back and was just hitting me . . . I finally got away from him . . . I couldn't exactly scream because everyone was home . . . so humiliating. I went into the bathroom and just locked myself in there and took a bath. By the time I went back to the room he was asleep or passed out.

Like I said, I can't wait for him to be admitted to the hospital.

Hi,

Sunday night. He wanted to go out. We went to The Depot. He was in a good mood. It's getting later . . . I tell him we have to leave. He gives me shit because he's going into the hospital on Tuesday and he wants to have fun. I let him alone. Finally we leave and on our way home he tells me he wants to go to Lou's for one more beer.

"Derrick, I am exhausted, I have two shifts tomorrow, I am taking Tuesday off to get you into the hospital. I am spent, I just want to go home and get some sleep."

"You are no fun! Jesus, listen to you whine. 'I have two shifts tomorrow.' What a baby. What about me? Huh? I gotta have surgery on Tuesday. You think I can't walk now. Jesus, Elin, I'm gonna be strapped into a full-length cast! Ya think you could just try for once to see it my way!!!"

"No. I really can't." I am so irritated at this point I abandon my fears. He speeds up and we are flying down Valley Road before it hits the River Road turn to Lou's, and all of a sudden he just slams on the brakes and pulls off into this empty lot thing on the left. He grabs me and drags me out of the car. He is completely a maniac and screaming about what a worthless bitch I am and he has me somehow on the ground . . . I am freaking out about me but also his knee 'cause he's on me and hitting me, then he's up and he's kicking me and then he's on the ground again and he pulls my head up by the hair and smashes my fucking head into the chrome bumper of the car. He must have hit my head three if not four times. I was flailing, trying to get away from him, but he was like an insane person. I managed to break free but felt faint. I fell and then I heard him say something like, "OH MY GOD, WHAT HAVE I DONE?" and he comes over to me. But I was just crying and he snapped again and started screaming that I am a fucking faker and then he grabbed me by the neck and started choking me.

"HEY! What the HELL IS GOING ON HERE?" There was a guy coming. "HEY, HOLD ON THERE, I'M CALLING THE COPS!!!!"

OK, I guess it wasn't an empty lot, it was a guy's house. Derrick hissed at me to get the fuck in the car, which somehow I did and then all the streets were whizzing by . . . Palmer Hill Road, Still Water, Cold Spring . . . and all I can think about is why didn't I just die . . . why . . . why couldn't he have just killed me. Cold Spring Road . . . how appropriate, maybe he can drown me instead.

Dear Derrick,

I just left the hospital and I can't get the image of you out of my mind. You looked so little and helpless and the contrast to how large you can become makes my head spin. They wheeled you into the room and your eyes opened and looked right at me. You were somewhere else, a drug-induced stupor. I watched as your lids, too heavy, collapsed upon themselves. Once the nurse adjusted everything I sat and held your hand for a while. The heart monitor bleeped in time to the beats of your slumbering heart and I inspected you from head to toe. You looked so peaceful, as if all the cares in your world had somehow been erased and there on the edge of my chair I wished it were so. What if those doctors could fix you beyond the repair of the knee? If by some miracle, by merely having been "put under," you could wake in a state of amnesia, a state that would arrest your demons and liberate your goodness. Who would you be? "Humpty Dumpty sat on a wall / Humpty Dumpty had a great fall / All the King's Horses and all the King's Men / Couldn't put Humpty together again."

Every so often you would twitch or move and I felt somehow powerful enough to take care of you. Soothing the crinkle that appeared between your eyebrows . . . adjusting the covers to keep you warm. When I left you, you still were in a fog, with parting words of love and appreciation for me. I dangle the thought that you are at my mercy in front of myself like a child with a yo-yo. You will be home soon.

I THINK MOST of us looking back on our childhood could say that at some point we had uttered the words, "I will never behave like that, do that, inflict that when I am a parent." In turn, I am beyond certain that I have broken every one of my golden rules and crumpled up each of the "Instructions to Self" yellow sticky-note reminders I've made, chief among them the need to remain emotionally available at all times, and never put my own needs above those of my children.

When I was in the hospital for my hysterectomy and finally able to stand without assistance, my first unaccompanied triumph was a trip to the bathroom. While washing my hands, I nearly fainted when I noticed who was staring at me in the mirror.

Later Jimmy came to visit.

"I had the scariest experience today," I told him.

"What happened?" he asked, trying to sound nonchalant.

"Who, not what. It's *who* I saw in the mirror." As is typical of him, he waited patiently for me to spit it out. "I saw my mother." I watched him try to cloak his amusement. "Seriously, it is so *not* funny. I looked just like my mother, as if I were seeing my future. There she was and to my absolute horror, it was me! Do I seriously look like my mother?"

His smile broke through his thin lips. "What?" he said.

"What? You ask me, what? Do I really look like my flippin' mother?"

"Yeah, you do." He laughed out loud. "It's not like that's a bad thing, is it?"

As I age it becomes ever clearer that I resemble her. On one level, I have to agree with him. My mother is far more beautiful than I am and the shadow of her reflected in my bone structure leaves me wondering if I underestimated my looks while I obliviously skipped through the pre-wrinkles and gray hair stages. But this thought leads to another: Am I *like* my mother?

After Jimmy bid me farewell I found little else to occupy my mind than my mom. Many years ago she sat post-hysterectomy, too, yet I have no clue what she felt or what she thought about at that time. Not once did it occur to me to ask her.

Alone now I drift back in time to our waterfront home.

"Mom, may I use the cushion from the chair by your desk?" We are at the dining room table. Our dining room chairs are the most uncomfortable things imaginable. It is a wonder that we spent countless hours at that table discussing the ways of the world. I can still feel the way my nearly petrified butt pushed into the rush seat. I remember coveting the cushion she attached to her own dining room chair.

"No."

"Why not?"

"Because I work there."

"But, you aren't working right now."

"No, you may not."

I press on. "What is the big deal? I'll put it back after. It's just for dinner." At the time she was working as an editor and I am quite certain she was up to her eyeballs in a manuscript. We can both sense our heels digging into the hard oak floor lying beneath the Oriental rug. I see her eyebrow challenge me to argue and I respond in kind with my own look. Like mother, like daughter.

"You are so selfish!" I say. As soon as the words are out I can see the flutter of a wince on her face and with that I feel the sting of tears in my own eyes.

Now my mind jumps forward to the misunderstandings I have had with my own children.

"You never answer your phone!"

"I do, too."

"No, Mom, you don't." Max's crystal-clear, light blue eyes bore into me. All traces of boyhood erased, he is left with the chiseled features of the man he is becoming.

"Max, I am in meetings the majority of the day. I do my best. I am not sitting at my desk in an office alone. I am in meetings. Was it important? Look, I really am sorry."

He stares at me, and it all comes back. Jimmy has told me countless times that I never answer the phone, I am always late, and that our family is on the back burner. "Whatever, Mom. You never answer your phone, that's all I am trying to tell you."

"Whatever, Mom." Not really words a mother longs to hear. I devoted years to climbing the ever-elusive corporate ladder in the male-dominated home-building industry and made every mistake imaginable along the way, particularly where my kids and husband were concerned.

Did my own mother feel pulled like a rubber doll in different directions? Did she simply need to claim her space? I can picture her desk set up in a corner of the living room with a water view and no doors to lock her away from the family and, yes, I can picture that chair and its cushion—her spot.

I am struggling with the fact that my work derailed me and consequently I was absent. Lots of people juggle career and family. Who is it I really see in the mirror? I am not my mother and my mother is not me. The year leading up to the surgery, saying good-bye to the physical capability of motherhood, I consciously reclaimed my place in the lives of each family member. Tugging on the sheets I am acutely aware that there is a difference between being home and being available on a deeply emotional level.

Obsessing about turning into my mother is another version of leaning on an excuse of why I am the way I am. It shifts responsibility from my shoulders to hers and that doesn't work.

Hi,

Ugh!!! Mr. Rhoades is such a prick!

We were both at the hospital today. "Hi Mr. Rhoades, it's nice to see you today. How are you doing?"

"Well, I'm just fine, Elin, nice to see you too. Well, I see you're helping to take care of my boy here."

"I'm trying."

"Well, my, Elin, you're looking a little thin these days. I sure hope you aren't dieting."

(Is he really that out of touch? I am thinking.)

"Uh, no, I'm not dieting. It's pretty much called working two jobs."

"Yeah, Derrick here was just telling me about that."

"Dad, can you just cut the BS, please?" Derrick is staring at me now and Mr. Rhoades is staring at him.

"Elin, I was just telling my father here how much you are working and how we could use a little help until I'm on my feet again."

"Well, yeah, Derrick, ya know, that's what social services are set up for. You two should maybe look into getting some government assistance . . . what with you on your back and all, they can't turn you down."

I was fuming!!! I don't know what came over me but all the manners my mother enforced got lost in the world of "government assistance."

"You know, Mr. Rhoades, that's not how my parents raised me. There are no handouts and, maybe this will come as a shock, but I'd rather starve. Derrick, I'll see you tomorrow when it's time to discharge. Call me at work. John knows I have to get you and he'll give me the time off." With that I gave him a kiss, and for the first time in my life, I left a room speechless! I wanted to punch the wall. Of course I didn't but what an asshole! I am still pissed about it. The guy has more money than he can spend and he tells me to go get welfare.

Fuck you!

———

Hi,

I brought Derrick home today and this is going to be rough! He is so happy to be home and so far he has been a jewel—best behavior. He's still all bent out of shape about his dad and what happened yesterday and it's like we are both on the same side in our rage.

He pretty much is sticking to our room over the next week. The cast is a bear and his knee really hurts. The pills help but it still throbs with pain. I feel really bad 'cause he will be just stuck in bed with the TV and everyone else will be at work all day. I won't be able to even bring him dinner 'cause there's no time to stop between jobs. Not that I get dinner either. Drew said he'd stop by here and there to keep him company, and so did Mike. I can make him some food before I leave in the morning so at least he has something. Anyway, the doctor said that in a week he will be a lot stronger. I sure hope so! I can't imagine being stuck in bed like that!

Hi,

Well it's been a little over a week and he is stronger now—but he doesn't always show it. I have been super attentive to his every need and I think he kind of likes that—great. So, he has been cleared to drive, which is way better than being stuck home all day. We had to switch cars though 'cause mine is an automatic and he can't manage the clutch in his truck. No big deal—I actually kind of like it. Before his surgery I had never even driven his truck. He always said how much he hated the way I drove—didn't trust me to keep it on the road or some bullshit like that. Gee, how sad. Guess he'll have to get over it 'cause I am in the driver's seat now.

Hi,

The days drift into nights and morning dawns without a dream. I pull out of the driveway onto Cold Spring Road five days a week to head to work—today is no different. There's that split second where I have to get the truck across three lanes to pull a U-turn. There are a ton of cars filled with industrious-looking professionals; like me, they are in that zone of getting from point A to point B.

I flip the U-turn and have to drive back past our house. Without fail I find myself trying to keep it in sight as I go by. He's in there sleeping. I don't need X-ray vision to picture his routine. The road curves and my eyes shift to the rearview mirror, but always the house shrinks from my view. I am occupied with picturing him getting himself up and the way his hands rub the sleep from his eyes and then rub his nose, a reach for Abby accompanied by a murmur of good morning meant just for her ears. He'll hoist himself up and make his crutch-supported trip to the bathroom and back. Once back on the edge of the bed he'll mindlessly grab a cigarette, light it, and while inhaling deeply, pull the knob of the television and watch other people's lives pop into his world. Maybe he looks at the empty space I left behind me and wonders how I am. I question, does he re-cast our latest struggle? Does he stare at that space and wonder about my day . . . or does his hand stray under the covers and reach for the miniscule bit of heat trapped in the sheets? Would he put his face in my pillow searching for a trace of me . . . a hint of leftover fragrance from my shampoo that separates me from anyone else, a scent lingering to remind him that I exist? Does he stand and maneuver his way to the window and seek confirmation that I truly left?

After I have parked, I need to collect my bank image, scattered like pennies on the floor of the truck. I am the friendly face that customers know by name. I know they like us, Sue and me. They linger in our company to see if our stand-up comedy will leave them with a chuckle. I glimpse my reflection in the rearview mirror and push it so I can't see the shallow, gaunt existence it reveals. All the people I am stand before me now, as if I can pluck what I need like a uniform off the dashboard. No, not the girlfriend. No, not the daughter. No, not the sister. Like the attendant at the dry cleaner, they spin past me and I slow the mechanism as I see my bank persona come into view. Deep breath . . . bank person. Bank mask in place, I leap toward my day with sarcastic remarks already prepared, like little barbs that explode into laughter.

Hi,

Mom called me today. She said she found a great school for me, just a little college tucked in the hills of southern Vermont. She's got a brochure, wants me to see it. I feel her tugging on me to stop by and look at it. Sure, I tell her, I'll get by today. It's Saturday and I have time. I fill the phone line with my schedule at the bar, a shift that begins at 4:00 p.m. She invites me to lunch. "Yeah, that would be great." I know she expected a no and I hear her enthusiasm through the receiver. I hang up with her promising to get there around noon. I tighten up my nerves to tell Derrick.

For a change, he is happy to release me. He thinks he'll head over to see his grandfather, do I want him to drop me off? No, I have work at 4:00. He will be free to tack on a trip to Gary's without needing to get me back *to Stamford. He likes that . . . my consideration of his freedom . . . he in his unencumbered life. He is in his good day and I rest easy with my secret agenda to preview a brochure that could take me away.*

In the shower I think about Mom, the idea of school, my jobs, the few friends I have at work, and how right this second I feel good. I try to picture myself at school, working on papers and sitting in a classroom. It feels so removed yet not all at the same time. I think about Derrick, will he ever have a real job, will I always have to pick up the slack when it occurs? A black cloud covers my mood and I lean up toward the streaming water . . . it pours down all over me and I wish it could wash over my memories, pour them down the drain.

Hi,

The cast is still with us. The weight of it rests heavy on my mind . . . I am still washing his hair in the sink and my duties feel endless. This routine has wound its way around me like barbed wire. It's never good enough . . . I tug . . . I pull . . . the water is too cold . . . the shampoo too much. Complaints oozing from him like sweat.

Hey,

Evil lurks at my fingertips and I am in shock over what I did last night. Bent over the sink with his leg balanced on a bucket, I am listening to his banter about my inability to wash hair for the zillionth time. I glanced down at him, eyes closed, lips moving, and I fake a move for the towel, trip, and kick the bucket with mean-spirited intention. BAM! The impact of his cast on the tile is deafening but not quite as much as the scream of agony that escapes his outraged face. I apologize with empty words and inwardly smile at what I am identifying as growing power.

Hi,

The slides I have in my head are stuck in the carousel. Almost unwillingly I click them forward and backward, adjusting the focus on the screen . . . is that me? I zoom in but there is so much blur to contend with . . . manual focus hones in on me, bent over in agony. CLICK, there I am happy. We are all at the races in Montauk . . . the motorbikes speeding past us. CLICK. Camping, too many beers, sun burnt fun. CLICK. Holding him in my arms I try to brush away his torment from his past. It's like sap, it sticks to us, unwilling to lose its hold. CLICK. He's threatening to dump a pot of boiling water all over me. CLICK. Laughing at Lou's . . . even Lou joining us in our reverie. CLICK. Driving in the truck, nestled next to him like conjoined twins, he plays with the inside of my leg as if he is a spider, a smile stretched over his face. CLICK, Abby's head in my lap, intensely wondering why I am crying. CLICK. Stuffed again in a bar, his hand on my back marking me as his own. CLICK. Playing pool over at Drew's, swapping jokes. CLICK, The Tombs, on the back of Mike's motorcycle, Derrick pops a wheelie in the parking lot, I am on the ground with a bruise already forming that will take months to fade. CLICK. The back of another buddy's motorcycle speeding through the dark, missing a stop sign and landing in a pile of rhododendrons with me screaming at him, "WHAT THE HELL IS THE MATTER WITH YOU, MY GOD, YOU DIDN'T EVEN STOP!!!!!!!! WHAT, ARE YOU TRYING TO FLIPPIN' KILL US????"

"Elin, one thing, OK, I know I screwed up."

"SCREWED UP? UNDERSTATEMENT OF THE CENTURY!"

"ELIN, one thing . . . "

"WHAT!!"

"Could you help me get the bike off my leg?"

"I SHOULD LEAVE YOU HERE. MY GOD, YOU SCARED THE CRAP OUT OF ME." Still spitting insults I lean over to help move the motorcycle off of his leg. I realize I am trembling all over.

We push the bike back up to the street and I swallow my urge to hit him. We climb back on and speed away into the darkness, a single headlight casting its beam ahead of us. The double yellow line borders the lane, screaming at me, "DO NOT PASS!" Do not pass . . . do not pass . . . do not pass go . . . go directly to jail. The board game sweeps through my thoughts and I wonder if I really ever was a little girl. I close my eyes and pray he gets us back to the party in one piece. CLICK.

I HAVE A scar that runs three inches across my abdomen. If I trace my finger along it, it feels smooth to the touch. Over time it should fade but because it is still new it almost appears like a grin. The body is amazing in its power to heal. The operation lasted two hours and while I was in my oblivious drug-induced haze, Jimmy waited in the designated holding room. Although I cannot crawl inside his mind and know how he felt, he has told me.

Vulnerable.

Is that not the essence of love—to cherish, let go, and render oneself completely vulnerable? As the minutes ticked by and the anticipation of news jumbled around in his belly, he was given pause to consider what he holds so dear; all that, the enormity of what he values, lying beneath the fingers of a surgeon. Clearly when the doctor made her entrance, assurances spilling from her mouth, he was relieved. I do know him to be a praying man and he no doubt uttered his own version of thanks to a God his own wife questions and argues with daily.

Seventy-nine days after my surgery I could run, jump, tickle . . . I could do anything. Conversely the recovery course that I have been on since my relationship with Derrick has not been so easy. I am a formerly battered woman, a statistic of sorts, a survivor. I was talking with my friend Karen, and she asked, "Do you ever wonder about how different your life could have been?"

I hardly even paused to consider her question and went directly into my assumption of what I thought she meant. "Yeah, it scares the crap out of me . . . if I married him and had kids. I can't even go there."

"No, no, that's not what I meant. Of course that would have been awful but where I was going is, what would your life have been like had you *never met* Derrick."

Now there's a question. Of course, it is what I refer to as mental masturbation. Yet it is an important question because I realize how much my life has been shaped by the fact that I did meet him. Of course, we massaged a few "what if?" scenarios, Karen and I, after which I indicated that what I should have done was to take a big-ass life insurance policy out on the bastard. We laughed, and she knows I am deflecting the *what ifs* with well-honed sarcasm.

Derrick did die. I learned about his death while I was living in Boulder, Colorado with Hunter, when we were still married. Closing my eyes now I swirl these memories around and trip over my imaginary gravesite for Derrick. I can picture the inscription as if I had been there to see it. There may be an epitaph that reads "loving son," or something to that effect. I close my eyes and reach out to the cold stone. "I forgive you, not what you did, but *you*," I whisper in my mind. I have the benefit of time, the distance of a life of recovery. He was a boy. He was an angry young man. He was a victim, too. I open my eyes and trace my scar again—evidence forever imprinted on my skin that once bulged with the new life of each of my babies.

Hey,
Mom and Dad are taking me up to southern Vermont to see the school Mom found. I haven't told Derrick yet and I am really scared to, he will never understand.

Mom already set an appointment with the admissions office for next Friday. I cleared it at both jobs and both my bosses thought it was really great that I was looking at a college. It is amazing how there are people who believe in me . . . both John and Michael. Really? I mean they have a work relationship with me, I report to them. And then there's Derrick. Is it not a given that love supersedes your own need and desire? Have I not sacrificed countless things to stand in support of him? And yet he has supported none of my interests. What am I doing with him? Seriously. Maybe this is the test.

Hi,
Just as I thought, my conversation about school did not go well. Test? Failure.

"Why do you want to look at a school in Vermont? What's wrong with Connecticut? Why do you even need to go to school? I don't get it."

"That's what I am trying to tell you. The school is really small. Look, I haven't even seen it yet. We're just looking at it, you know, checking it out. It's not like I am for sure going. Besides, it's not like we can't still be together. We just wouldn't be living together."

"I sure as shit don't want to move to Vermont, so how the hell can we still be together?"

"I wouldn't even ask you to move to Vermont!"

"I just don't get why you need to go to school. What the hell is wrong with the jobs you have?"

"You're kidding, right?"

"No, I am not fucking kidding. Why would I kid about that?"

"You really think I want to work in a bank for the rest of my life—I don't even like math! Or serve drinks to a bunch of drunks? I think I can do a little more than that."

"Oh, that's right, here we fucking go, it's always about how smart you are, huh? You think you are smarter than me, huh? Is that it? Answer me, huh? Is that it?"

"No, you are twisting my words around."

"I AM TWISTING YOUR WORDS? OH, OK."

"Look, I am checking it out. Get over it. Why can't you want something for me? Why does it always have to be about you?"

"That's right, yeah, everything is so about me!"

"Yeah, actually, it generally is, Derrick. I want this. Why can't you just be supportive? I really don't get it. And I am done talking about it."

"This isn't over. I am not done discussing this. I tell you when it's over."

"Nope. Done. I gotta go to work."

I turned away from him and left to go to work.

I pretty much shut it out but then at around eleven he showed up at the bar.

"You can't be here, you know the rules."

"I'm not gonna bother anyone."

"No!"

"This is a public bar, Elin. Call the manager, have him kick me out."

"If I lose this job 'cause of you I swear to God we are through. Last I checked you weren't working and we need the money."

"Oh, now we need the money."

I walked outside and he followed and I could see Summer watching me like a hawk through the glass.

"Derrick, look, you have to go. I really don't want to lose this job. The rules are simple. You have to go home. We can talk later."

"You really can be a bitch. Fine, I'm out of here."

I just turned my back on him and went back into the bar. Just as I walked through the door, I saw Summer put a full Red Hook on the wait station for me. I walked toward her. The place was pretty well dead tonight anyway.

"What's with him?"

"He's all bent that I am looking at that school next week."

"Ah, jealous."

"Pretty much."

"They're all pretty much assholes, Elin. Don't let him stop you from going for your dreams."

"No, not anymore, Summer. I hope to hell I like the place and that I get in."

"What does he do for work anyway?"

"That would be a big flippin' nothing right now."

"Hmm, sounds like someone doesn't wanna lose his meal ticket."

"God, I am stupid."

"No, no, Elin, seriously don't go running down that road. Look, I don't know you too well. You know you don't really talk about yourself. I notice that stuff. But I can tell you, stupid you are not."

"If you really only knew." I slugged my beer. "I better finish the clean up and get out of here."

"OK, sidestepper."

"Sidestepper?"

"Yup. People who dodge questions, I call them sidesteppers. You, my friend, are a sidestepper, and on top of that you get everyone else to talk about themselves."

"Wow, I guess you do have it figured out, Sherlock. Gotta go."

She just smiled.

I put my mind to wiping down all the tables and organizing the condiments and other busywork, all the while turning over how I was going to deal with Derrick. By the time I got home he was plopped downstairs, surrounded by our housemates, beer in hand and barely a greeting on his breath. Good, another dodged bullet.

———

Hi,

This week has been a mess. Derrick's been pretty much a prick and the bar has been quiet, which means I have been home earlier. Hate that. It's late enough that he's been drinking and early enough where he paws at me and whines about how I am leaving on Friday with my parents. The whining always turns into a pissing match about why I want to go to school, and I am wishing I had never told him I was going to Vermont at all!

———

Hi,

Slow shift again but tonight rather than go home, Summer and I sat in the bar and talked over Red Hooks.

"OK, sidestepper, spill. How'd the school tour go?"

"Well, Sherlock, it was actually great."

"And?"

"And I am applying."

"You go, girl!"

"Yeah, huh, pretty amazing. I still have to get in, you know."

"You'll get in."

"What about you, Summer? What's your path?"

"There ya go again, girlfriend, but OK, I'll humor you. The answer is travel. You know I make my money in the strip joint, not really here; this pays the bills but the other? Future lifestyle."

I sit there and really look at her. Stripper? I just can't totally wrap my mind around it.

"Where do you want to go?"

"You name it, Elin, everywhere . . . everywhere but here."

I can't stop thinking about Summer, now that I am alone. She seems so set on what she wants. I admire that in a way. But I also am wrestling with this nagging sensation about my little dust roadmap. I think I have an exit in college, and I keep praying for back roads and detours that take me to a way different road. A road away from here, from him, from this, from the me I wake up to. I am so angry with myself and how I got here. Self-loathing is percolating.

Hi,

Bad night . . . really bad. He started in again the second I got back from The Boat House. I swear I hadn't even taken my frickin' shoes off.

"Oh well, if it isn't the cocktail waitress, the college student. What are you going to major in, huh?? Hmmm, I bet she'll major in . . . let's see . . . sex education." He grabbed me and pushed me onto the bed. "You little fucking slut, you gonna screw the whole campus? Huh, is that it, all the hippy fuckin' burnouts? Is that what you like, huh, the bearded hippy types? Birkenstock-wearing fucking hippies."

I buried my face in my hands. I am so tired, was all I could think. He kept going on and on about how I was into having sex. Finally I snapped, like really snapped.

"Yeah, yeah, that's right, you pegged it! I'm going to college to further my knowledge in sexual encounters . . . you know, sexual encounters of the real kind. Yeah, that's right. How's it feel, huh? You suck in bed!" I shoved him back and he lost his balance a little bit and fell backward. I stood back up over him and yelled at him.

"What is with you, huh? What, you dropped out of school in what . . . ninth grade . . . huh? Is that it? So what? You're gonna punish me, huh? Punish me 'cause I didn't? Is that it? WELL, FUCK YOU!"

I left the room and went downstairs and into the kitchen. There was Carter. I started cleaning the dishes for something to do. As I was cleaning, I started singing. I was singing "Dirty Work" by Steely Dan.

"Elin." I jumped at Carter's voice.

"Yeah? Jeez, you startled me."

"Sorry. I just feel I have to ask you something."

"Yeah?" I dried my hands. "What . . . anything . . . what's up?"

"The song . . . well . . . it made me wonder. I mean, you actually sound like you mean it . . . the not wanting to do the dirty work . . . so I thought I'd get up the balls to come out and ask you . . . when are you gonna leave?"

"Wow. Guess I wasn't expecting that."

"Yeah, well, the walls are thin and he's a prick."

"Right . . . ."

"Listen, it's probably not my business but I hope you do . . . I really hope you get out. He really doesn't deserve you."

"Thanks, really, that's nice. I am super confused, ya know? I mean I love him but he can be so jealous . . . and not just jealous of people but jealous of me . . . ya know? Does that make any sense?"

"Yeah, but here's the deal . . . he's not going to change. You? You are changing."

"Hmm . . . thanks." I whisper 'cause I hear Derrick coming down the stairs.

"No problem."

Derrick walked in as if nothing had happened. He wouldn't look me in the eyes but I could tell it was over for tonight.

"I'm going to bed," I tell them, and with that I leave Derrick to Carter's glaring eyes.

WHEN HUNTER AND I reconnected after my relationship with Derrick was over I was still very fragile—to me he was another would-be hero—only this time we had a history. In the infancy of our love we commuted back and forth between his college and my apartment in Greenwich, a distance that served only to fuel our desire to be together.

Within ten months we were married and, both having abandoned school, headed to the White Mountains of northern New Hampshire to begin our married life. Hunter and I each stood sentinel to the swift unraveling of our marriage. Candidly I could fill an entire book about our marriage, but I won't. What is important to know is neither of us welcomed the idea of raising our child in the middle of what turned out to be our many irreconcilable differences. Max deserved more—and so did we.

The decade of my twenties was a slow waking up for me. Having a child provided a new lens to look through, a microscope of sorts that upon deeper scrutiny revealed all the bacteria of my past. I had never really been alone, and my attempt at defining myself through the eyes of others was no longer an option.

We managed five years of marriage before filing for separation and in that time we ping-ponged back and forth between desire and rage. I know my first husband to be a good man; he is not violent or cruel. He loves his son and for what they share I am grateful.

Putting my marriage to rest for me was excruciating; really it was a death. I had to mourn the dream of what I thought it was going to have been. On many levels I had to walk as many steps backward as I had forward in order to extricate myself from the ruin—and that journey, like so many, began with packing.

"I'm down here, Mom!" I hear her enter the condo that belongs to my in-laws. I am planted on the floor of the basement and look up as my mother descends the stairs.

"What on earth are you doing, dear?"

It's so familiar, my mother's voice. In an odd way I wish I could climb back into her lap and cry, but too many years have been swept under the rug for that.

"Sifting through memories," I say, trying to guard myself from breaking down.

"Oh, Elin, I really don't know that you should be doing that. I thought you were packing."

I thought you were packing. The words hang between us and I feel as if I am hanging by my fingernails from the edge of a very tall cliff. Apparently I have been packing . . . for years. Each issue is carefully wrapped in old newspaper marking the time, hours, days, months, years, decades; all nestled together with the expectation of being stored permanently. Insecurities, heartbreak, jealousy, torment, misunderstanding, anger, all packed into the box marked "No Need to Open." Yet scrawled onto worn-out sheets of yellow legal paper are pieces of me pleading for me to unpack.

Mom approaches and sits on the couch nearby.

"Any insight?" she asks.

"Oh yeah, startling really. I suppose I really hadn't stopped to gather all of these loose pages—the letters unsent to Hunter—into a pile, you know, to force a read of my thoughts back to me. And now, here on the floor, surrounded by heaps of despair, I am sitting here thinking, 'Well, no wonder we are separating.' No wonder."

I look at her, my mother, and I see understanding flicker behind her blue eyes. She is staring at me and I wait. She is clearly processing what I have said and I have the sense that she has something to add. Minutes tick by. "Mom?"

She casts her eyes to the floor and she grabs her wrist where her signature bracelets dangle. "Well, Elin, I was thinking about how very brave you are."

"Brave? Me? You have got to be kidding."

"No, I am not kidding. It takes incredible strength to uproot. You will be fine dear, you are a survivor."

My mother's words dangle in front of me. I am a survivor. The weight of the inference is unmanageable, and without saying a word I think about her own choices. She stuck it out. It couldn't have been easy to raise five children, bury one, move twenty-five-plus times, and for better or worse stay with my father.

"You sound like you're masking regret, Mom."

"Oh, there's no time for regret. I still have times when I want to run away. I tell Bomber we should just run away."

"Bomber? There's company, Mom. Guess it's no mistake that Saint Bernards are portrayed as heroes with booze strapped around their necks? Should I remind you now that he drools?"

She laughs with me, but in her laughter I believe I hear something more. Is it regret, resolve—or neither? And as fast as I hear it, it's gone. As our laughter fades, I know that whatever I heard is hers—not mine. "You will be fine, Elin, I feel it in my very bones."

"Yeah, we'll see. I mean, I get why this is happening, but I am devastated. Let's start with what this is doing to Max. I mean, he stays with me and all but he loses his dad! I keep asking myself if I am doing the right thing by moving all the way to Colorado."

She is quiet.

"But then I think of what our being together is doing to him—all the fighting, it is constant. I don't want Max to grow up thinking that is normal . . . or that one of us is the enemy. As if that's not enough, it's not just my marriage I lose here. I also lose his whole family; they have become my family, too, and I just know it will cut like a knife. His mom, his dad—I mean, his sister is one of my very closest friends. I am so scared to lose all of that. It feels like a death, only I feel like I am the cause of death!"

And with that, my last fingernail gives way and I am falling fast.

"Elin, I really think for your own sake you need to focus on packing. All the backward glances aren't going to change where you are right now. So it may be best to clean up the papers, photographs . . . " She waves her hand at the mess I have made. "And set your mind on your purpose."

She is right in the literal sense—the time I have to complete my task is limited—but on an emotional level, I question whether I have the strength to continue shoving everything inward, layer upon layer. *Or if I should.*

We downshift into small talk and I pretend to be cleaning up the papers but really I am sorting them, still compelled to continue down the path of memory. As Mom and I say good-bye, she offers to bring Chinese food for dinner and we agree to meet at the end of the day.

Once alone, I return to the pages. The handwriting is frenzied, sloppy, almost illegible. I can picture a former version of myself bent over the page but really I have no sense whatsoever of when or where, I only know it was months before we were married and at the time we were hopelessly in love.

Hi Hunter!

I miss you!!!!

It's a damn good thing my dad lives in Colorado 85 percent of the time 'cause I wouldn't be able to live here if it were different. Hunter, I am trying so hard!!! Like never before . . . open, honest and every time I turn around. It's like my dad's trying to make me out as a liar. He will not let go of my past. It so sucks and hurts. I am so upset and totally do not get it!! He has no respect for me. All he has is snickering comments and I am sick of it! He acts like I am forty or something and like I ought to have it all together. It makes me feel so incompetent or useless. It's like he thinks I will never amount to anything. You know I have tried so hard since I left Derrick to relate to my father, ask him for help, ask him for advice. Hunter, I never took a penny from him when I was living with Derrick. Not one lousy penny. I busted my ass, worked two jobs . . . never asked!!! And now it's a big deal for me to live here.

"At 21, you shouldn't be living off your old man!" Oh my God, I sooooo felt like saying to him, "Yeah??? Well where was my 'old man' when I was 17, 18, and 19 and we won't talk about 13, 14, 15, and 16, will we, Dad!!!!"

"Elin, you don't really want to go to school . . . it's a myth!" Why? Why does he say things like that? It only hurts me.

We got into this stupid-ass argument 'cause I asked to borrow the car to pick a friend up from the airport. He nearly jumped down my throat "It's not your car!!!" I never said it was!!

I am sorry, I shouldn't be laying all this on you but I need to talk to someone. Usually I just blow off his remarks but he actually came right out and said he didn't trust me. We were talking about the debt I incurred while working at the bank. I make my payments. I got into debt without him and I'll get out of debt without him. I made some comment like I'd never want to inadvertently screw him by not paying it back. You know what he said? "YOU ALREADY HAVE SCREWED ME!" What???? HOW??? I have never asked him to co-sign. Never would. No matter how hard I try I can't live up to his expectations. It sucks.

I love you so much, Hunter. You love me for who I am. You make me feel worthwhile and valued. Again I am sorry to dump this on you. I would call you but it's his phone!!!! I miss you so much. Let's move, I want to move. I just want to be with you and live away from here.

Wow. I vaguely remember that argument with my father. It seems so odd now. The whole rage is incongruous to how things are right this minute. I am trying to remember what it was like to feel like Hunter loved me for being me and that he once valued me enough to say so. Was that the way it was? Or was that what I needed to believe?

I shuffle the pages like a deck of cards and find another equally disturbed-looking pen scrawl on a yellow page. It's just one line:

Hunter, What do you want me to do/be?? What is it that's so incredibly wrong with me??

Maybe Mom is right. I abandon the scraps of despair and instead pick up a stack of photos, countless baby pictures of Max. Dozens of captured moments; there are the early ones when Hunter and I first fell in love and we both look so happy. As the years carve away the joy the images reveal an absence of feeling . . . like a vacancy sign in an old, worn hotel.

Hey!!!

I just heard from Mom. She opened the letter while I was on the phone at the bank. I got in! Oh my God! *They accepted my application. I, Elin, am going to college!!!!!!!! I am so excited!!*

Hi,

So that went over like a lead balloon. I mean, what did I really expect? That he would celebrate the news? He just stared at me for the longest time, not saying a word, just looking at me.

"What?"

"What? What? If you are waiting for me to congratulate you, you are go-ing to be sitting for a l-o-n-g time."

I think I just shook my head. Not sure. Uncomfortable . . .

To me,

I am at Mom and Dad's, sitting on my bed looking around what was once my room. My parents finally went back to bed. Oh man, this is ugly. It's nearly 1:00 in the morning. I honestly question if I will sleep tonight.

He lost it. We've had our battles but honestly I thought this was it. I got off work around 11:00 and went home. Of course he was already in our room; the glow from the TV was visible when I pulled in. He must have turned the light on between my parking and walking up the stairs. When I walked in the room he was on the bed, beer in his grasp and several emp-ties cluttering the table. I actually thought about turning around, and how I wish I had. As soon as I was in my sweats he began the pawing routine that recently has become a habit.

"Stop. Seriously, I am beat."

"What the hell is wrong with you? You never put out. What; you think I have no needs, HUH? ANSWER ME, BITCH!"

"Get off my case. Any thread of desire for intimacy has been pulverized by your attitude. Get away from me, you repulse me."

"I repulse you? Oh, now I've heard it all . . . you know you are worthless . . .

"That's it, I am so done with you, I am out of here!" As I tried to get up he grabbed me . . . oh my God, it was so awful I almost can't begin to write this. Somehow he was hitting me all over and I was trying to break free and also hit him back, I finally broke from him and managed to get up off the bed on my side.

"I AM SO OVER YOU!!!! I HATE YOU!!! I AM DONE!!!" I was sobbing and screaming at him and trying to grab some clothes.

I turned to see him lock the door and he stood there and said, "There is not a fucking chance you are walking out of here alive." He walked toward me and I could see the limp left over from his being in the cast . . . closer and closer . . . I started backing away, which only cornered me back by my side of the bed and then he was on me all over again. Pushed me back onto the bed and was just hitting me everywhere. He managed to pin me down and was straddling me. He held my wrists by both hands and was inches from my face, saying things like he was gonna get what he wanted out of me even if he had to force himself on me. He was trying to kick my legs apart and I was thrashing. He then somehow transferred his grasp to one hand on both wrists and with his free hand he grabbed a pair of scissors that were on my bedside table. He held them up above me . . .

"I'm gonna fucking kill you!"

I could hear pounding on the door—BOOM—BOOM—BOOM—"DER-RICK, OPEN THE GODDAMNED DOOR!!!!"

He grazed my face with the scissors and then drew them up again. "You've had it, bitch . . . "

"DERRICK, OPEN THE DOOR!!!"

"GO AWAY, CARTER, THIS ISN'T ABOUT YOU!!!!"

BOOM—BOOM—BOOM

His eyes are bulging. The door snaps open with a cracking sound and

Carter hauls off and coldcocks Derrick right in the face. Out.

"Elin, get the hell out of here!!!!!!"

Not stopping to grab a thing other than my purse and keys, I hug Carter and peel down the stairs. I jump into my car, rev the engine, and scream onto the pavement, flipping my U-turn before the signal granted me permission.

When I reached my parents house I went straight to their bedroom, "Mom . . . Dad . . . "

"Elin? What's going on here?" I could hear Dad clearing his throat the way he does when he's worried.

"Dad, I just wanted you to know I am here, I am home. Sorry to wake you."

That wasn't going to work. He was out of bed and to both our horror he was naked. He was grabbing his robe and I went to my old room.

I was crying uncontrollably. "What happened? DID HE HIT YOU??"

"No," I lied.

"Are you sure?" He was inspecting the cracks in my armor. "Elin?"

"Dad, no, we just had a huge fight. I can't deal with him. It was too much tonight. He's all bent about my going away to school in January and we had a falling out. I need to move home, OK?"

"Of course it's OK. In fact, let me get dressed and we will head back there right now, we'll get your belongings."

I could hear Mom coming up behind him now—thankfully, I thought, she can help me calm him down.

"Bob? What's going on? Elin?"

"That SOB is giving her a hard time about school!"

"You guys, I am really sorry. Can we just talk in the morning? Seriously, Dad, I need to finish this thing myself. I can drive over there tomorrow and grab my stuff. I can't live there anymore . . . it just isn't working on that level. Really, let's all get some sleep." The fear I had of my dad's involvement was sobering my need to cry. They both finally agreed and retreated to their bedroom.

I can hear the rise and fall of their voices from behind their closed door and I know they are discussing me. It makes me sick inside to think of the worry that was scattered like dust particles across their faces.

Shit, what a mess. He threatened to stab me with scissors . . . are you flippin' kidding me? Not leaving alive? He is insane. I am beyond *understanding him. I can't handle this . . . it's too much. What the hell would have happened if Carter hadn't busted the door in to help me? I'd be in the hospital, or worse—the morgue.*

———

Hey,

Well, I did it. I went back over to the house and grabbed all my stuff. Derrick wasn't home when I got there . . . thank goodness! Drew happened to show up and he helped me gather my things. Not like I have a lot. Right when we were done throwing it all in my car, Derrick pulled in the driveway. He got out and walked toward me and I just shook my head.

"You got what you want, Derrick. I am taking my worthless self out of your life."

"That is not what I meant and you fucking know it." He was seething.

"You could have fooled me. You tried to stab me, or have you forgotten already?"

"Derrick, her old man knows she's leaving. Just move the truck and let her go."

"Drew, this doesn't involve you."

"Sure it does man, both of you are my friend and I love you both, too. Seriously man, just back the truck out of the way and I'll take you out for a beer. OK?"

His eyes were downcast and I could tell he was falling apart. I had to bite my lip for fear of crying now, and my hands were shaking.

He finally turned around and got back in the truck. He pulled it out of the driveway and then blocked traffic.

"OK, that's it then. Thanks, Drew, you are the best. I'll catch up with you later."

"You bet. Hang in there, E. It will all work out."

I got in the car and backed out into the lane where Derrick was frustrating the people who had to get around him. I looked in my rearview mirror at him and his expression revealed nothing. I pulled away and ever so slowly inched my way across traffic for yet another U-turn in my life. As I drove by I could see the truck had been re-parked and he and Drew were standing in the yard watching me pass. Drew waved but Derrick, he just watched and despite the fact that he was no longer visible, I could feel his eyes on my back the entire trip to my parents' house.

Yeah . . . but does he see me?

———

Hi,

Carter kicked Derrick out the day after I left. He is now living with his grandfather, who is such a sweetheart.

We've talked on the phone a few times. It's only been a week. I can't manage to keep from crying. It's not like crying in the way you do when things hurt you personally. It's more like a response to his anguish. I mean, how am I supposed to manage this? Each time I talk to him he falls apart crying. Over and over he keeps apologizing . . . telling me he can't be without me . . . it's killing him.

Killing him? I keep telling him that I need a break. School is in less than two months and I need to figure out what's happened between us. I reminded him that he told me I wouldn't leave the room alive . . . his words . . . not my words. How the hell am I supposed to "get over" that? He just breaks down. This is so hard . . . it just totally sucks.

———

Hi,

It's Thanksgiving and I am holed up in my room right now. I can hear the family in the other room. Rod's got his guitar out and he and Lorna are singing. My heart is breaking. How the hell can I miss him? I am having such a hard time being around the family . . . it's like I am outside looking in. They all seem so happy. They are glad to be together but I wish I could just crawl away. No one has any idea what I have been through. I feel like the seed head of a dandelion, bracing myself for being plucked and blown into oblivion. They would be shocked.

I am so depressed. I am trying so hard to focus on going away to school and remember all the horrible things he did. But even when I try, I also think

about all the good times and how much he says he needs me. It's so con-
fusing. What if he does hurt himself or, worse, kill himself, Abby, or me. The
worst part is sometimes I really miss him.

I found a note on my car this morning. It said "I love you . . . give me an-
other chance." At first I thought, chance? This isn't like a bet, or is it? Maybe
it is like Russian roulette. A chance to make it different or a chance to finish
it. Another chance. Do I just throw two-plus years away? Chance . . . what
kind of a chance does he need?

HAD I HAD the ability to be a spectator watching my life with Derrick unfold in a movie, I would have wanted to scream, "Leave," "Get out," "Save yourself!" I am convinced of it.

I know now I need to live in a way that doesn't ever leave me wishing later I had screamed.

Hi,

He showed up at the bank today. I saw the truck pull in the parking lot and Sue looked over at me with question marks all over her face. I walked over to her. "What do I do?"

"What do you want to do?" She looked me over and I know she has no idea that he is violent.

"I don't know what I want. I really miss him . . . but then not all at once. My God, I am off to school in January. I have no idea what to think about that."

"He's standing in the door . . . he's looking at us." I could feel my hands shaking and I tried to calm myself without any luck.

"You are going to have to turn around, I don't think he's going to leave."

I know she's right, so slowly I turn to him, and I walk to my drawer, lock it, and let myself out from behind the locked counter. As I walk to the glass doors I am trying to tell myself to stay strong . . . don't give into him.

"What . . . what do you want?" I pull him off the door stoop and walk toward the truck. "Derrick, I am working . . . "

"I know, but I can't stand it. I can't make it through another day. I mean it, Elin, I need you so bad, baby. I can hardly eat or drink." His eyes are rimmed with tears and I feel like I'm on an amusement park ride that won't stop spinning. I want to scream for someone to get me off of it but I can't even breathe, I can't find my voice.

"Baby, you gotta believe me. I know I did and said really bad things. I was depressed—the whole surgery and everything, it totally fucked me up. You have to believe me. I can't lose you . . . seriously . . . I really can't lose you. Look, I know you need to go to school and I am proud of you, I swear to it. I've been talking to my grandfather and he's really been telling me how if I want to be in a good relationship with you I need to get behind the things that make you feel good. I know he's right but it's like torture for me thinking of all the people you'll meet . . . I just am dying thinking that you will meet

someone else. Elin, please, you gotta give me another chance."

There's that word again. I feel my head continue to spin. Seriously? I have heard all this before. I reach for his arm.

"Derrick, you know I love you. This is really difficult for me, too, but it's impossible for me when you tell me you 'can't live without me.' That's just not right . . . ya know? I mean you have to love yourself more than that. It makes me feel too important for you or something. The rest? It's words. I have heard all these words before. Hollow, empty words. I need space . . . I need to think."

"Whatever you want, just give me a chance. I will walk away if I try to hurt you again . . . I swear. The words . . . they aren't hollow, I swear to it."

"I gotta get back to work. I can't just make a decision like this without thinking about it."

"OK, please. Abby needs you, too. We love you, Elin. You gotta come back to us."

"Derrick, don't, OK? I gotta go . . . "

I walk from my grasp of him, feeling my resolve fade before my own eyes. Back in the bank, Sue's eyes follow me back behind the teller station. I grab my stool and sit down. She walks up to me.

"Well?"

"He wants me back . . . you know? He really can't let go of me. I just don't know what to do. I mean sometimes I just feel like I will never get away from him. I mean he can be so sweet but sometimes . . . .well, he can really be hard to live with. I just don't know . . . maybe if we aren't living together . . . maybe that will help."

"I don't know, Stebbins, sounds complicated."

I look up at her. "Yeah, more than I can say . . . "

Hi,

So I guess we're back together. It's all different. I mean, he's at his grand-father's and I am over here at Mom and Dad's. I quit my job at The Boat House. It was too much. I really miss the people but I was tired all the time. I am trying to create more boundaries with him—like not going to the bars every night, and eating with my parents, getting home at 11:00 if we do go out. Also I won't let him drive my car anymore—I either meet him or I drive. I can tell he's biting his tongue trying to not make mean comments about how I drive. He used to always give me a hard time before, but he is really trying.

The whole thing is making Dad insane. He is not happy that I am spending time with him, at all, told me he doesn't trust it.

"Trust it? What do you mean?" We're in the basement by his desk and he's seemingly cranky. I see his jaw push forward and he is shaking his head from side to side.

"Dad?"

"I don't trust you to keep it at a distance. You have plans to go to school, I don't want that clown interfering with that."

"Dad, I admit it was really bad the night I came home . . . "

"I'll say. I don't like it, I just don't like it."

I am a bit at a loss. He won't change his mind and right now I am grateful to have his support and help. Getting in a pissing match about Derrick isn't going to help him think about it. Mom seems to get it. I mean, I don't think she's overjoyed but I think she is just trying to remain neutral or something, almost as if by fighting me she could push me back to him. She has just been patient. She has told me I seem tired and that worries her . . . but not in a nagging way.

It's so weird being here, I mean really, it is surreal. I am caught between being a child and being an adult. I am so used to not telling them a whole lot and not seeing them and now, well, they are around all the time. Is it ever too late to let your parents care? In some ways it's kind of like too little too late . . . perhaps for all of us.

I KNEW GETTING back together with Derrick was a risk, but I was bargaining in order to reach a decision that was not as painful or definitive as the one that needed to be made. The bargaining began with promises I made to myself. These promises went something like this: he promises to keep his temper under control and I promise myself that I will be assertive, strong, and not allow any form of abuse. I had no idea at the time that this assumed I had power and control in the relationship. Essentially my own self-talk indirectly made me feel responsible for allowing the abuse—it took me years to realize that was false.

I wanted to believe him. I thought I loved him and I wanted him to get control of his temper because when he was happy, it was fun to be with him. His need for me was alluring, too. The mere fact that I was capable of negotiating with myself like this was a small step toward breaking through my denial. I was no longer pretending that it wouldn't happen again; I was taking tentative steps toward admitting it was a problem.

But I had not admitted it yet.

In my sketchbook from the years 1982–1983, there is a self-portrait. I am surrounded by bright pink and my face is completely shaded in. The word "BLANK" is written above my head, floating in the sea of pink.

Pages later, I wrote: *My self-respect has shattered again. How can you hurt me and then pretend to be my friend? How long do you expect me to listen to your promises? Just because you think you're right doesn't mean I am wrong. How can I? How can I? How could you?*

If I felt I had the upper hand, then I was keeping my promise to myself. When he was keeping his temper in check, then that part of the bargain was intact also. Once there was an incident—and there was always an incident, because without clinical help a batterer will not stop—then I would spin into self-loathing. Once he begged for forgiveness, the cycle of bargaining would start again, and I was once again caught in the web of denial.

Hi,

I am so worried about heading off to school in January.

    Things have been pretty good with Derrick. He keeps telling me that he's in it for the long haul and that even when I am at school we can keep it together. He gave me a ring; it's a band and I am wearing it but on my right hand. I feel like I can't just put it in a drawer 'cause I see him all the time. So weird, here all this time I wanted him to give me a present and he finally does and I don't want it, but I have to keep it. It's been kind of strange lately because I have been more in his face when we disagree and he has kind of backed off almost like I have the upper hand? But then every so often I hear him respond to me and it's like he's trying everything within his power to not snap. That's the eggshell thing I hate. I mean, I know what he can be and is capable of so I almost always feel on guard. It's hard to just relax and trust him. It's all so weird. He has gotten some work and usually when he has side work he isn't as short tempered.

    In some ways I just want to get to school so I can remember who I am without Derrick. He's so wrapped around me I almost feel like a mummy. But then I am scared to get to school because I worry I will not fit in. I mean, living in a dorm? I have lived on my own and I picture the people at school and wonder if it will be weird or what?

    I gave my notice at the bank and my last day will coincide with the end of the pay period. Mom and Dad both agree I should take the rest of the time to enjoy Christmas, New Year's, and then prepare to head off in mid-January. It will be weird not working.

Hi,

So much for Mr. Nice Guy—he is obsessed with sex. Ugh!

I can't stand it. I have zero interest in it right now; if anything I just don't want to be touched! He hasn't hit me or anything but it's a little bit, I don't know, edgy or something. Like last night we were at his grandfather's and he kept trying to touch my leg when his grandfather was in the kitchen and I was getting pissed and shoved his hand away and I told him stop it.

"What? I can't touch you?"

"It's embarrassing . . . he's in the next room . . . lay off!"

"What is with you? You are like an iceberg."

"No, I just don't appreciate the way you're touching me. It's not even affectionate. It's kind of . . . I don't know . . . makes me feel trashy."

"I make you feel trashy."

"The way you are touching me makes me feel trashy," I spat at him.

"So now I can't touch you, is that it?"

"I did not say that!"

"You don't have to. I get it . . . or maybe you're just playing hard to get?"

"Oh my God, shut up!"

Thankfully his grandfather walked back in the room and I shot Derrick a look like "up yours," not that he seemed to notice. I was so glad I had driven to the house and that he didn't pick me up.

"Thanks for dinner, Grandpa, sure was good . . . as always!"

"Sure, love having you here, sweetie, beats the heck out of all the testosterone in this house!" He chuckles at his little joke and I hug him. Derrick, of course, follows me to my car outside with his grandfather safely behind us in the warmth of the house.

"Wanna take a drive?"

"No. It's freezing outside. I just want to get home."

"You act like I am a disease."

"Why is everything so personal with you? I just am not into fooling around in a car, alright? It's gross!"

"You are so Miss Manners now. Whatever. Crawl home."

"You can't make me feel bad about this. I mean it . . . I won't. Don't call me later either, I'm going to bed."

"Like I would."

Puhlease! How about as in you always do!

"Sure, OK. Goodnight."

I ducked into the car and started the engine. He was already on the porch and turned around as if he wanted to say something but I drove away to leave him in his own spilt mess.

―――――

Hi,

I actually got together with friends last night, a bunch of people are back home from school and it was fun to get together. I went on my own without Derrick and he was a bit bent out of shape. But, like I said this newfound upper hand seems to be working. I kind of don't give him the opportunity to argue. So, for example, I called and just said I was going out with girlfriends and I'd see him the next day. He kind of just stammered like he wasn't sure what to do. I think maybe I used to put everything into a question or something, like "Do you mind if . . . ?" or "I was thinking maybe . . ." I am almost afraid of the way I am pushing him but then it makes me feel good so I just keep doing it. He seems really lost–confused or unsure. I think he must be worried about when I leave so he doesn't want to get me overly pissed. Or maybe he doesn't think about it at all. I feel like it's all I think about!

He told me today that Logan is having a Christmas party next week and he wants me to go with him. It's down in Belle Haven where Logan's folks live but I guess they aren't around. I don't know, I kind of wasn't following the whole thing, but I did say I'd go. He tagged on we would go together as in the same car. Fine, I'll drive then. Tonight I am meeting him at Lou's. I so do not want to get into the whole issue about sex again, so I hope there are other people there and I can just leave early!

―――――

Hi,

Maybe not working wasn't such a great idea. Now Derrick constantly wants to be together and he keeps saying how we won't be able to when I am at school. I feel like we are a record that keeps skipping in the same spot.

Anyway, he has been better, like last night he didn't give me a bad time when I left Lou's. He did make me promise him that we could go to dinner together tonight and spend time together, so now I am dreading it but not. I mean I love him and I want to be with him but the whole being touched thing is out of whack for me. Ever since that night on Cold Spring Road I can't get the image out of my head that for a moment he wanted to kill me.

Hi,

OK, so last night wasn't so great. We had dinner and everything was nice. I, of course, drove. He begged me after dinner to drive to Shady Brook Lane where the road ends and there are no houses and I know what he wants but then I was getting nervous 'cause I can't just keep telling him no, and God . . . I just hate myself! I feel like I am being mentally raped. I am the rag doll going through the motions but there is just nothing there for me; I just want to die. The way he gropes me? Everything and I mean everything in me is screaming to get him off of me, but I just consent, give in.

I thought if I just get it over with then maybe I can just go home. I mean, that worked and all but then he wants to talk and I am yawning and finally I say to him, I want to go home. This time he just got all sad and whiny—how much he misses sleeping in the same bed and waking up with me. Inside my head I am saying, "LALALALALALALALALALA," you know, like you do when you don't want to hear, see, or feel?

I got home and took a shower. I just feel like a used piece of garbage. Logan's party is in four days and I am not at all excited about it.

I AM LIVING in Colorado when my divorce from Hunter is finalized. It took a while but after months of separation, I finally start to feel at peace with who and what I need to be.

I am perched comfortably in the shade of a tree in the open space adjacent to my condo in the town of Gunbarrel.

"VROOM, BEEP-BEEP-BEEP." I can see Max's tongue peeking out as he positions his yellow Tonka truck.

"OK, Joe! Let it fly!" the little plastic man figure yells to the truck.

"RRRRRRR." Slowly the bed of the truck rises and I watch as the contents slip into a pile.

"Great job, Joe! You did it!"

I am mesmerized by his parent-words.

"Thanks, Mack! Off to get another load. You take care now."

The letter in my hand is urging me to open it. It is from Mom.

"Thank you again for your 'real letter,' and the flowered card. Could picture you on the train. One *sees* the country from a train. Can sympathize with you when the mom-and-five boarded. Under such circumstances, one simply *must* move, even if it means bursting, like Hercule Poirot, into some stranger's compartment."

I am chuckling now. In years past Mom was that very woman from whom others would escape. After all, she herself has five children. Did she notice the would-be Hercule Poirots not so gracefully bolting from her when she entered a room with all of us? Or did she want to be her own version of Hercule, the one who "*must* move"? My finger passes over the words and I note that she has underscored *must* and feel as if I have indeed solved a riddle.

The letter continues and my mother's voice is alive in my head.

"Also sympathize with your 'longing for sameness.' This is why I cling so to New Hampshire." Here we go. Now my own words from my "real letter" are streaming back to me with a mom twist: "I feel like Kerwin in *The Bone People,* when she wrote, 'Uprooted again . . . but I seek always for homes. I find, then I lose. And I am not a traveler at heart, just a casual gypsy wandering out from my base and back.'"

My parents are living in the house that Hunter and I renovated. Although I am in agreement that it is the best solution for them, I am feeling the implications for me. It feels somehow that my need for stability and "sameness" is being overshadowed by what she longs for, what she needs. The message I am receiving is that my mom wants to remain in my house, yet the words I read just fall short of saying so.

That house—we destroyed it and each other all at once. I wince at the memory of a crowbar smashing into the plastered version of our relationship.

"That's not how you do that," I hear him shout over the music.

"I'm sorry, what?" I say, pulling the air filtration mask from my face. The room is dense with plaster dust. I can hear our best friend Jeff smashing away at a wall in another room; he and I have been here all day tearing down plaster, pulling away lathing, while Hunter worked for a local contractor on someone else's house.

"The way you are doing that, it's all wrong." I look around. Were it not for the fact that I am standing on top of the demolition trash, I'd be knee deep in it.

"What do you mean, 'all wrong'? Are the walls down?" I can feel the first step of my trotting pulse preparing to sprint into defensive posture. How about, "Wow, good for you!" I am thinking.

I see his lips moving but the noise from the music and Jeff in the other room is competing with him and I find myself not caring. "I mean look at this, Elin, it's just piled up everywhere."

I toss my crowbar down and start following the noise toward Jeff. I round the corner and there he is atop his own rubble, wielding his own crowbar exactly as I had been for the past several hours. I gesture toward Jeff and see Hunter roll his eyes. I don't need to say anything; if I am wrong then so is Jeff. I glare at Hunter and walk away, saying, "Nice to see you, too." I pull my gloves off and throw them down by the front door and head outside.

Our house is at the very end of a dirt road that Ys. The population of Lyman, and its neighbor Lisbon together, hovers around one thousand. This is rural. As I sink into the quiet and beauty of this haven, I feel my irritation brush away with the plaster that I absently wipe from my wrists. Behind me I hear the guys.

"Hey, Baby, what do you say we head down to The Ammonoosuc's bar and grab a few cold ones, you know, shoot some pool maybe, take in a little country music?" The man I love has returned; his request is a hooded apology. His critical counterpart must have remained with the mess in the house. The unoccupied house fades in the rearview mirror as we peel down the dirt road in search of local camaraderie at The Ammonoosuc.

In the bar I glimpse my reflection in the mirror. My hair is covered in plaster dust and so are my jeans. Despite the shower I haven't had, I feel good, almost sexy. My muscles are sore, my cheeks are glowing with the third beer, and I turn to see Hunter leaning over the pool table. The crack of the cue ball sends his ball to the pocket and I see satisfaction twitching at his mouth. He winks at me and all my irritation is swallowed away by the intoxication of my pure attraction to him, and in that moment he knows he has me.

Unseen are the miles that stretch ahead, the unraveling of love. Standing on day three of "renovate the house," we are unaware that we will become parents—and that we will also slowly strip our relationship of the ability to forgive.

The fact that my parents are in the New Hampshire house creeps back in, pushing old memories back in time where they belong. There is a passive request in this letter. It is subtle, cloaked in the quote from the book I suggested she read. Again I feel it . . . it's as if she wants to stay in the house and despite my not wanting to be bugged, I am. It just doesn't feel fair. The house is now finished. The photographs show me trimmed windows, hardwood floors, paint. My parents' furniture makes it look inviting, familiar, loved. I am envious. My own associations are of projects left unfinished, a chore in every nook and cranny, worn-out plywood floors with ruts of disenchantment that Hunter and I fell into as if they were potholes.

My formerly battered self was not strong enough to manage a marriage; Hunter in many respects was another disguised savior in my life. I still had not figured out that I had to rescue myself.

So I left, I hauled all my belongings and our child 2,500 miles away from that house, and then went back only to discover that all our problems were still there.

Now as I sit under this tree back in Colorado, the ink on the divorce papers is still wet. But I am rediscovering pieces of me, the pieces I like.

"Mom, watch this!!!" I look up as he leaps to his feet.

"Wow! You landed on your feet! Like a cat, Max. Just like a cat, you will always land on your feet."

"Like a cat," he repeats, "always on my feet!"

"Ready for some lunch?"

"Yup!" I see him heading over to the Ninjas and overhear him telling them he's like a cat.

Dear Mr. Policeman who tried to help but will never ever hear from me,
Thank you for trying. I have no idea why I let you drive away. I could tell you care. Are you the only person who is concerned? God knows I must not be . . .
    From, I think,
    Elin

The word. He said, "Just say the word and I'll arrest him. I saw him hit you, Miss Stebbins, but I can't do anything unless you say the word."

The tension in the car is asphyxiating. Arrest him? I am shaking like a leaf and my head is pounding and I feel like I am going to throw up and pass out

*all at the same time. I can almost not hear him. "Miss? Miss Stebbins? Do
you understand? I cannot continue to follow you . . . you just have to give
me the word and I will drag him out of your car and take him downtown."
I look at Derrick and he is shaking his head no. I look up at the cop and I
swear he is only a little bit older than me and I can almost imagine him as
my brother, but then not, all at the same time . . . and I can't seem to say the
word. I shake my head and now there are tears rolling down my cheeks and
the cop looks like he is going to cry, too.*

*"Thanks . . . but . . . no . . . I'm OK . . . I mean I, we . . . we'll be . . . OK . . .
thanks . . . " I trailed off in a whisper, and he shakes his head at me like he
is in more pain than I am. I hear him utter some sort of good luck and how
sorry he is kind of thing and he turned and made his way back to the car
with the lights flashing to the entire population on Rail Road Avenue that
something was wrong. I see him in the side mirror strap himself into his seat
belt and he is still shaking his head and I can tell he will wait until we pull
into the lane before he turns the lights off. I hear Derrick . . . he is telling me
to get the motherfucking car in drive and go. There's my reward for saving
him . . . my purple heart . . . I do as I am told and I can hardly think.*

*The police . . . I can hear her, my mother, as in a dream from an eternity
ago, something about how she will never forgive me if I ever do anything
to tarnish my father's name. At the time I was just turning fifteen . . . I had
failed my tour in boarding school and West Hill High wasn't working out so
well . . . I think she knew I was partying or something.*

*Would this kind of mix up with the police count? But then they would
know . . . everyone would know. I am driving and Bruce Park is disappearing in the rearview mirror and I am incapable of hearing. My mind keeps
seeing the headlights and once again I am vanishing. I can't even see my
hands. I'm on the Post Road now . . . and he is still ranting, but at least he
isn't touching me. In what feels like the longest drive of my life, we finally
arrive at his grandfather's house.*

"Get out . . . .just get out . . . " I whisper.

"What?"

*"You heard me . . . get out." I can't even look at him. I hear the door open
and unbelievably, he actually gets out. I am trembling uncontrollably.*

"I said I'll talk to you tomorrow."

I just shook my head. Finally the door closes with a snap and I reverse the car, not waiting to see that he makes it inside. As I turn onto Sheep Hill Road I am beyond driving, and when I reach Mom and Dad's neighborhood, I pull over. There I sit crying . . . I cannot walk in the door like this. He tried to kill me again . . . What is wrong with me? Why would I let him walk away? Why?

My mind replays the events of the night and I want to shut it all out but I can't. I am that skipping record again . . . over and over again, and all I can picture are headlights coming at me on an empty road.

"Hey, are you about ready to head out?" I ask Derrick. There are a ton of people at Logan's party and we hardly know anyone. Some people are dressed up and I feel like I didn't get the invitation right. I just want to go . . .

"No, are you kidding? My God, lighten up. Have a drink already, huh?" He is incredulous.

"OK . . . alright . . . maybe another drink then we go, OK? I feel funny here."

"What else is new? You just don't know how to have fun anymore." His words sting but I shake them off like rain. This is just a moment; I have the upper hand.

"Tell you what, how about I get you a drink . . . and then we'll go in a little bit."

"Now we're talking . . . lighten up." I cross the room and pour him a drink and me a water. I cross back and hand it to him and then drift to see if I can find someone besides Logan and Sue to talk with. Not really. I circle through the downstairs and hope that Derrick is now missing my company. I find an empty sun porch and sit for what feels like thirty minutes. Maybe he'll miss me? Hmmmm. I finally leave the empty room behind me and search for him and our departure once more.

Out in the car he just starts his speech all over as if we hadn't had the extra time in-between inside. "Man, you need to drink more. Lighten up or something . . . loosen up, too. Jesus Christ . . . I mean, really!"

I shake my head as I leave the driveway and Logan's party behind. But he is on a warm up and I feel the knot in my stomach tightening.

"What did you have, one drink?"

"I guess . . . who cares?"

"Who cares? WHO CARES? I CARE! YOU ARE JUST NOT ANY FUN!"

"Look, if you're gonna raise your voice, you can walk home. We've talked about this. I am not up for your yelling at me." At this point we are upon Fergus's house up on the hill and I see it and wonder if that ever happened, if I ever had a relationship before Derrick. He's yelling at me still, but I am gone . . . we're past the house I want to just turn around to that time.

"Are you LISTENING TO ME????"

"SHUT UP!!!!!" I scream at him.

I am in control, me. I have the upper hand! *My head is spinning. Out of nowhere I see him pull the keys from the ignition. I can feel the power steering disappear and I do my best to get on the side of the road before the car rolls to a stop. Now I put the car in park.*

"DERRICK, GIVE ME THE FUCKING KEYS!"

But he slides from the car and is out in the street. I see him put the keys in his pants and, as he does, he grabs his crotch and yells to me, "COME GET THEM, BITCH."

The words are banging in my head, and I feel my "upper hand" slipping to my side and it is being sucked into oblivion by the demon I see in front of me. Slowly I get out of the car.

"Derrick . . . come on . . . just please . . . please give me the keys. Come on, I'm tired. I want to go home. It's 11:30 . . . please . . . "

"You are always tired!" He pulls the keys from his pocket and throws them as far as he can up the street.

I can see them and take off in a run toward them as if they are the answer to all my problems. As I turn from grabbing them off the pavement, I see him in the distance. The hood to the car is up and he is pulling something off. He turns to me with a car part in his hand and smiles but not a nice smile and chucks the thing into the bush.

I start running toward him now, and I feel my desperation mounting. "DERRICK, PUHLEASE, LET'S JUST GO HOME. WHY? WHY DO YOU HAVE TO BE LIKE THIS????"

I am pleading, and he grabs me and twists the keys from my hand and I can feel the rage in his grasp. RUN. I twist from his grasp and start running, and all the while I am wondering where the hell am I going. And then I hear it, there is no mistaking the rev of a V-8 engine. Oh my God, no! And I am running, and I can see the lights catching up with me, and my head is yelling at me, RUN! I can hear the car and jump to the side of the road and I swear to God that motherfucker almost hit me. If I hadn't jumped . . . oh my God. RUN! HE ALMOST HIT ME? RUN! I see the car squeal to a halt up ahead and flip a U-turn and now he is coming back at me, and I am in the middle of the road again. I hear myself screaming like a wounded animal.

"NOOOOOOOOOOOOOOOOOOOOOOOOOOOOOOOOO!!!!!!!!!"

He swerves to his right and up onto the side of the road and screeches to a halt again. Now he's out of the car and coming at me on foot.

"YOU COULD HAVE KILLED ME!!!" I am running straight at him and just start hitting him. There's a contest. He has me pinned in minutes and is beating the crap out of me and I am SCREAMING, with my face squished into the dirt. I see the flashing lights coming around the bend.

"GET UP! It's a fucking PIG!" He's off me now and pulling me up. "GET IN THE CAR!" We are getting in the car as the cop is pulling up and Derrick is telling me to be cool. I am in the driver's seat. How did I get here? I am having a hard time choking back my tears. The cop is walking to the car and I see him motion for me to open the window. Deep breath . . . .

"Hi, officer?"

"License and registration, please. There was a call that there were screams and some yelling. Miss, are you alright?"

"She's fine, officer," Derrick informs the policeman.

"I'M NOT ADDRESSING YOU," the policeman sternly tells Derrick, his voice raised.

"Miss?" I can see his flashlight on my license and there's no question that he saw my shaking hand. "Miss Stebbins?"

"Yeah? We had . . . we had an argument . . . but . . . no . . . it's fine . . . thanks . . . " He tells us he needs to call in my license and walks back to his car. Derrick is repeating to me that I need to be cool . . . don't fuck him over . . . he's had enough with the Greenwich cops . . . be cool.

"OK, Miss Stebbins, everything checks out. Are you sure you are OK?"

My mouth won't work. It's like someone took my voice. I nod yes. He stands there like he won't leave until I change my mind. He leans down into the window. "Get a hold of yourself," he says to Derrick. That kind of wakes me up.

"Thanks, officer, really, it's OK." I tell him we need to turn around and head back in the other direction, and he says fine. After he is in his car I pull out and into the road and pull into the street just before Fergus's driveway. I use the street to turn and the policeman does the same, following me. As we are driving, Derrick is yelling at me. He starts pushing me and hits my arm a few times and that's when the cop pulls us over again, on Rail Road Avenue, and for the second time this evening I let the enemy escape.

I finally stop crying and I feel as if I could sleep for a decade. I have to get home. As I pull into the driveway I see only the study light is on and I feel relief that Mom and Dad are in bed asleep. I creep into the house and crawl into my bed as if it were a church.

To Whom It May Concern:
Another day has passed and you know what, dear-person-who-is-perhaps-concerned?

I do not give a shit!
Call me a cynic, call me what you will 'cause
Sticks and stones may break my bones
WORDS FOREVER HURT ME.
I AM RESIGNED to the fact
That one day that SOB will KILL ME,
And Damn Nation Under God.
I pray he does 'cause he will be left
With no one, just a body.
You don't have me.
Not as I know me.
Not as people knew me.
Don't call me Elin.
I am the mere illusion of a human being,
Just a puppet—a mere marionette.
You the puppeteer;
Hold those strings tight, puppet man,

For should you drop them
You will see
Me fall, SPLAT.
The people who knew me
Will cry for Elin.
Yes, dear person who perhaps is concerned,
Tonight he tried to kill me,
And if anybody asks,
It wasn't with a gun.

———

Hi,

I think I cried the entire night; I am so unbelievably sad. I am sequestered to my room in an effort to avoid Mom and Dad. Mom poked her head in and asked how I was and I told her I was feeling kind of sick . . . understatement of the century.

I cannot stop thinking about last night. Derrick of course called me . . . like I really want to talk to him.

"Hey."

"What do you want?"

"I want to talk to you."

"I honestly have nothing to say to you."

"Come on, babe, don't be like that. I love you, you know that."

"Yeah, funny you say that, Derrick, but you have a really warped way of showing it. And do NOT call me Babe."

"Hmmmm. . . . yeah, about last night . . . "

"No, you aren't getting out of this. You fucking tried to hit me with my car!"

"No I didn't. I would never have hit you."

"This is exactly what I am not willing to do with you, Derrick. I am not listening to you re-write history. How many times have I listened to your apologies? Huh? I am so done. I cried the entire night. Do you even give a crap? I doubt it. I bet you slept like a baby."

I could hear him breathing.

"See? You can't even respond! I actually hate you right this second. I can't even talk to you. My God, you lost it last night! Don't call me again today. I can't deal with it . . . not even a little bit."

"Elin, wait! Don't hang up!"

"What? What could you possibly dream up to say that I haven't heard before? You . . . you are like that little boy who cries wolf, but YOU'RE THE WOLF!!!!!! I HAVE TO GO!!!!"

"No, seriously, hear me out!"

"I AM HANGING UP!!!!"

I can't leave the phone off the hook because this is my parents' house. He better not come over here. He called me again but I hung up on him as soon as I heard his voice. He probably won't try for a while 'cause he is afraid of drawing attention to himself as far as my parents are concerned. If only I could be this strong when he is in front of my face! The phone makes it way easier!

———

Hi,

I agreed to see him. It wasn't the two million phone calls. It was the note:

Dear Elin,

I know you are really upset but I am sorry and I will do anything to make it up to you. You leave for school in less than three weeks and I cannot go without seeing you. You know I love you. Please, I am begging you. I need you and want to make this up to you. I love you forever.

    Derrick

P.S. Abby wants to see you, too. This is her nose print right here.

That was in my car with a flower. I caved. I don't know how to deal with him. He just falls apart crying and I feel like I am holding a newborn baby and threatening to drop it in a trash can when I tell him I just can't go on . . .

———

Hi,

What started it was the picture I drew of myself. I decided to draw a self-portrait, after I literally stared at my reflection for almost thirty minutes.

I pulled the mirror off the wall and put it down on the ground and without really examining myself. I just started to draw. It's when I finished that I was startled enough to stop, put the paper to the side, and stare.

I hardly recognized myself.

Last fall I checked out one of the cameras from school to try taking pictures. The one thing I noticed back then was looking through a lens is really different from just looking. The lens is so small that it forces the eye to choose what it sees. Then, with precision, the hand needs to focus the lens so that the camera actually snaps what you want it to. This is what it was like for me today looking in the mirror. While I was drawing I was just part of the reflection but once I put my pencil down and looked at the drawing, then the captured image all came into focus.

The girl I drew . . . I don't know her. She is worn like leather, joyless, spent, ancient. I forced myself to look at the mirror. The thing of it is . . . it's not as if I am frowning and angry. What is scary is I look vacant, gone, dead.

And that's when it crept into me . . . he really can't kill me . . . well, he could, but that's not what I mean. What I mean is, he actually already has, because he's killed my spirit. This is what it means to be alone, really alone . . . because there is not a living soul who I can tell.

I hardly tell myself. He must feel me slipping because he has asked me a million and one times if I really understand he won't live without me. Now that I know I am dead, how can I care about his life? After all, he is the creator of what I see staring vacantly back at me.

I had to stop. I found a small blanket in the hall closet and covered the mirror. Then I had to leave my room. I was trembling. I walked to the kitchen and grabbed a snack, then I mechanically went into the living room and sat down by the huge window that looks down the Mianus River. I drank in the view . . . all the deciduous trees were bare. And that's when it hit me with full force. All those beautiful trees, they shed everything that makes them gorgeous and they endure the long, harsh New England winter and then just when people almost give up hope, they sprout their tiny little buds. A month or so later they have leaves; some have flowers too.

I am nineteen and I am the tree. I am almost unrecognizable, yet underneath the twigs and sticks and bark there is a strength. I can feel this strength. I don't want to be dead among the living. That tree would no sooner refuse to sprout than fall over if I pushed it. Maybe . . . at the core . . . maybe I am still here.

So I got up and went back to my room, pulled away the blanket, and sat back down and again gazed into the mirror. My eyes are green . . . somewhere in the pool of black squarely centered in all that green is a path back to me. If I stare at it long enough maybe just maybe I can see deep inside and find my core, my strength, my light, my spirit. It's winter but sure as day will turn to night, spring will come.

"I am alive . . . I am alive . . . I am me and I am alive."

ENDING MY RELATIONSHIP with Derrick was a series of awakenings. The college I went to was less than 200 miles north of my hometown. It quickly became a haven. It was there that I realized how jumpy I was. Everything—and I mean *everything*—startled me. In the beginning I think I half expected to see him around every corner but when I didn't, it liberated me to just be.

What I remember the most was the pure exhaustion I felt; fatigue that no amount of sleep would cure because it inhabited every cell and beckoned me to climb into bed, sleep a dreamless sleep, and wake up to a reminder of what life without fear felt like.

In this rural Vermont community, I searched my soul for every ounce of strength I could muster . . . and slowly I emerged from the devastation of my pulverized life. One of the effects that abuse had on me was that I

12/82 SELF PORTRAIT

lost trust in my own judgment. I was paralyzed when faced with making even simple decisions. I also distrusted what I would offer to anyone as a friend. I felt diminished, and therefore being attractive on any level felt as remote as a Kansas cornfield.

When I first arrived at the school there was a guy who set his sights on me. When Charlie first acknowledged that he was attracted to me, I was floored, I really couldn't understand what he would see in me. My response was to prove to him how damaged I was and it ultimately drove him away. My mind was spinning from the barrage of phone calls from Derrick. Over time I plotted my escape from his hold on me, but I did so without the benefit of knowing what a safety plan was. Most deaths occur within seventy-two hours of a breakup. I was blind to the danger I was in; truly I am fortunate to be alive. I recognize that today cell phones and social media have brought a whole new dimension to abusive relationships—access that never ends: a stalking tool. Young people must be taught that electronic devices can be used as either a tool or a weapon.

Derrick,

What would it have been like if you weren't so angry deep down inside? I wish sometimes I could crawl inside your head with an eraser, like you were a huge chalkboard. I could erase everything and then color in new pictures for you to grow on. Like a dot-to-dot, listing all the steps you needed to follow. There are sides to you that I wish I could bottle—your laugh, your silly jokes, your love for Abby, your love for me—the soft side.

I love you so much but then when Hyde shows up all that gets shattered, and it's me on the ground with the hand broom picking up the shards of glass . . . and I am covered in cuts and dripping blood. What do I do? I place the broken-up pieces deeper into the landfill of my life, walk to the sink, rinse the blood, and root for a bandage that will hide the scars.

Love, Elin

LATELY, RUNNING HAS turned into a four-letter word. I suppose it is because my back has been hurting because I am cemented to my desk chair sifting through my past. While sorting through the journal notes that have led me backward, I have allowed the world to melt away like snow on a warm day.

For a change in routine I text-messaged my friend Colleen: "Any interest in a run/walk?" to which she responded: "Yes." So rather than going rearward I laced up, ready to take a leap into the now.

The incredible fortune I have in friendships with women is beyond measure. There is something about the safety and trust forged in each relationship that is like a great escape into a place where anything goes. Share it like it is: professional ups and downs, kid triumphs, kid worries, joys, fears, frustrations, the occasional husband grievances, and physical ailments. Whatever, you name it, no holds barred.

Like me, Colleen has had the same car for the entire twelve years we have known each other and seeing her familiar van rolling up the street is like watching a life raft arrive.

We walk through the gate that will take us away from my neighborhood, and we immediately launch into an exchange of the mostly mundane occurrences in our respective lives. Before we know it five miles have clicked by. I love her company and am grateful for her willingness to talk without pause on the hills that make me pant and want to die. Listening to her work out the details of her life is a welcome break from all my life sifting.

A great deal of my retrograde motion has been focused on Hunter. It has taken one hell of an opener to pry the lid off the can of truth about how I felt when my marriage ended. All the scribbling notes I saved have taken me back in time to the reality that I folded into my heart.

Hunter,

You know, it seems like you have no clue about what I feel. You are so focused on your own pain that you assume I'm not feeling anything.

You don't feel the knot in my stomach when I go to sleep and wake back up. You haven't seen me toss all my dreams out of the now-shattered proverbial living room window—dreams that included being your wife, your friend, your lover. Gone, tossed, ditched, pitched. They all have been spent.

Everything, every little thing with us is a fight, an argument, a conflict. A game of "Let's see who can hurt who more." We have lost the ability to even be courteous or respectful. I am exhausted from trying to explain what happens to me emotionally when your words tear me down. I can't and won't perpetuate the feeling that has taken over me. I have been through enough. Seriously, what would happen if I actually believed some of the things you have said to me?

As a mother I cannot fathom our son growing up with the two of us as an example of marriage and love. Look at him; he cries every time our words cut like a knife. I was in Max's classroom earlier and all the kids had drawn pictures of their families. Page after page of little stick figures holding hands and smiling. With an eager heart I looked for Max's. There it was, three little stick figures all standing apart from each other, no one touching, Max is alone and upright and you and I are sideways, faceless. In the car alone, I cried. The loss cut so deep I felt I could not breathe.

But tonight you tell me I don't feel anything? You tell me I am an unhappy person. You tell me I will never be happy. Again I ask, what would be left of me if I actually believed you?

Not only do I not know the you that you have become, but I do not know the me I am turning into. Scared, sad, lonely, and very insecure. And you know I promised myself . . . I promised I would never hit this bottom again. You may not be hitting me with your hands, but your words take my breath away.

There was me, there was you, and there was that third prong called us. Is this true of all couples, married or not? What do we build and believe to be the sanctity of our relationship? In our case we forgot that it was sacred. We forgot to cherish . . . We forgot.

It's over, really over. I do love you, I just am not in love with us. And for a while I think I will be dying inside . . . and then I will be alive again.

Elin

Hey!

I'm at school and my roommate seems really nice. Her name is "Stacey," nickname for Anastasia. She's what people would call "perky," talks fast with a lilt in her voice, the absolute opposite of me. The room is great; it's big and it has a decent view of the woods.

I am kind of in the zone, unpacking and listening to this girl chatter on and on about how great everything is going to be. I can't stop thinking about Derrick. The past few weeks were OK, but I feel somehow lighter here. I promised him I would call with the dorm number, so I s'pose I need to do that. More later.

Hey!

It's been, I guess, a week now? Wow, time is flying. Derrick, so far, is driving me nuts. He calls every night. The phone is way on the other side of the dorm and I feel kind of bad for the girl whose room is next to the stupid thing. He wants to come up here, and I am so not ready for that. I think he's going to be here next weekend . . . Ugh.

Hi,

Distance has not made my heart grow fonder. I am so not into him. I really need to just break up with him. I am obsessing over all this and it is really hard to concentrate. The whole weekend was just one big argument . . . and he was only here one night! Stacey actually slept in a friend's room for us, but I almost wish she hadn't. The last thing I wanted was to sleep with him, but I did. I am empty . . . words don't really begin to describe it. Somehow since I have been here at school I can't stop thinking about all the horrible things he has done. I feel like I am waking up from a coma and slowly seeing things clearly.

Great. I am in here writing and there's a knock on the door that the phone is for me. Of course it was Derrick.

"Hey, what's up? How was the bus home?"

"Sucked."

"That's too bad. I kind of like the bus; then I can read and not have to worry about driving. A real bonus is if I fall asleep."

"Whatever."

"OK? Is something wrong?"

"Yeah, something's wrong. What are you, stupid?"

"Jeez, I'm not staying on the phone for this bullshit. Why the hell did you call if you are in a crap mood?"

"I can't handle this. This whole thing, it's just fucked up."

"What 'whole thing' are we referring to this time?"

"Jesus, Elin, what the hell is that all about?"

"LOOK, YOU CALLED ME!"

"No shit, I thought I wanted to hear your voice."

"Yeah, well you did. Later." I hung up. Screw him!

Of course the phone rang within seconds.

"Hello?"

"Elin?"

"WHAT?"

"DON'T EVER HANG UP ON ME!"

"What are you gonna do about it? Huh? Guess you'll have to go punch

a wall 'cause I'm not there."

"Jesus Christ, you are a bitch tonight!"

"You know what? Fuck you!" *I hung up.*

Of course he called again.

"Hello?" I mean it could have been someone else. After all, there are a lot of people in this dorm.

"WHAT IS YOUR . . . "

"I am done. *You know what? I want out. Don't call me . . . seriously. I can't do this. I am hanging up and I am telling the girl in the room next to the phone that I won't take your call. SO DO NOT CALL BACK!"*

"What the . . . "

Yeah, stick it. Slam the phone down.

So I am sitting here praying he won't call back. So far he hasn't. What an asshole.

Hi,

I am beyond the ability to focus. Derrick is sucking the life out of me and he isn't even here. I swear to God it's almost like going to the movies every time I close my eyes to think about him and I'm not talking a good movie . . . more like a horror movie. Why is all this stuff happening now? I feel like I am being stung by bees in my head.

I can hardly get myself out of bed. It seems like every time I sit on this tiny single bed it just pulls me into sleep. I have got to just go home and end it. He calls all the time. It's almost like the conversations bleed into one another. They are all exactly the same as the last. He always has to tell me that it's not working for him to have me so far away, I get defensive, he yells, I yell, I hang up.

Angry. Angry. I am so incredibly angry. Red? You think you see red, Derrick? I'll show you red that will blind you. It's inside me like an infection that's crept into my heart. I stop to feel it with my right hand. Thump, thump. Thump, thump. But my fingers can't detect it, all that balled-up anger. It's not at the surface, though I feel it deep down. It's eating away at my vital organs.

Hi,

Now it is the pleading phone call that morphs into the assault of insults. I swear I could just rip the phone off the wall. He just doesn't get the fact that there isn't an Elin for him to be in love with anymore. He whittled me into something else. I don't recognize her to be me, I honestly don't know who or what I am. How will I ever love anyone else if I can't find myself inside to love first?

Hi,

Ugh, there is a guy here, Charlie. I suppose we have been doing the flirt thing. I am really not in a great position to go out with another guy, so I guess you could say it was all pretty benign. I actually am so frightened to even think of what I would attract right now in my life. He pretty much gets off on being the mysterious type, which is fine since for me it's all going nowhere anyway. Until tonight that is. Apparently he is more interested than he likes to let on . . .

I was in the library trying to get work done. Yeah, Friday night on campus; normal people are partying. I am so not into partying right now, so I went to the library to get away from the noise and just bury myself in the quiet of the stacks. Charlie shows up. We actually ended up lying on the floor next to each other talking . . . kind of the way you would if you were on a blanket under a sky with stars. Just the two of us in the entire library whispering among the books. He kissed me . . . I kissed him back . . . it was nice. Of course now that I am back in my room, my head is throbbing over Derrick and all the noise in the dorm is not helping. I have to go home . . . it's like I can't stand it anymore, if I don't end it in person he will just continue to call me and ruin my life. This bizarre thing with Charlie tonight kind of woke me up to an old memory . . . affection minus fear.

Hi,

That's it. I am heading home first thing tomorrow. I don't even care that it's Valentine's Day or that I will miss classes. I have to break up with him. I don't think I can handle another one of these stupid phone calls. It is a complete and utter embarrassment to be yelling into the phone. The girl who is next to the phone, her name is Jennifer and she feels really bad for me. Thank goodness, *since she is constantly coming to get me for a phone call. Tonight after I hung up on him for the third time, I poked my head in her room and told her how sorry I was. She told me it wasn't a big deal, that it wasn't like I was the only one in the dorm with a stalker for a boyfriend. She said it with a smile so I know she isn't being mean. I told her I was gonna head down to my parents tomorrow and hopefully put the whole thing to rest.* Yeah, like in a coffin nailed shut!

Hi,

What a totally fucked up two days. I am exhausted, completely used up, nothing left, out of air. I really don't know if I can cry anymore. I look like total shit.

I did go home and I did not tell him that I was on my way. Mom and Dad were surprised to see me. We had dinner at Tracks—quite possibly the most difficult dinner I have ever had in my entire life. I had asked them to not let Derrick know that I was home and, of course, Dad gets bent that I am trying to involve him with anything that has to do with Derrick. Well, ultimately, I had to just put it all out there. I basically projectile vomited the whole story over dinner. I thought Dad was going to leave the restaurant and go hunt Derrick down or something. He pounded his fist on the table, and everyone in the place turned and looked at us—well, me! They probably thought I had done some dumb thing 'cause he said super loud how it was "unacceptable behavior." *Uh, yeah . . . that's one way to put it! Anyway, I have to say my parents were actually pretty great. I mean, once they heard me out and all. They are probably in a state of shock. I feel really bad about that.*

Anyway, so after dinner we went home and Mom and Dad went to bed, I was hanging out watching TV in the study and I heard his flippin' truck. I darted to the door and into the driveway. He was already out of the truck.

"You can't be here, seriously you have to go."

"Happy Valentine's Day to you, too . . . what the fuck? . . . "

"Nice mouth. How did you know I was home?"

"Well, let's think about that, smart one. I called you at school to say 'Happy Valentine's Day' and the chick who answers the phone told me you went home to Connecticut. Nice. Like, how about a phone call? Huh?"

"I was going to call you tomorrow."

"Well . . . save yourself the trouble . . . I am here right now."

"No, you can't stay . . . I mean it."

"Elin, it's bloody cold out here. Let me in, let's just talk about this."

"Alright . . . alright . . . but you have to be quiet. My parents are asleep."

"ALRIGHT." He barked to my back and followed me into the warmth of the house.

We sat down opposite one another and I struggled to find my words, "I don't know where to begin."

"Here we go . . . I feel it. You think that now that you are in school you just don't need me, like I am some fucking ball and chain."

"Not my words . . . but yeah, I can't do this anymore . . . the calls . . . the past . . . It's all just a mess for me, I am cracking . . . I can't deal . . . it's too much for me."

"No way. I will not just let go of you like that."

"Derrick, this isn't about what you want. This is about what I want or, in your case, what I don't want. I don't want you . . . us. No more. I don't have the strength. I have been falling apart and it scares the shit out of me."

"No way. I will not just walk out of here with this . . . no way . . . this is not over . . . " He actually clamped his hand on my knee and I jumped so fast out of my chair that I surprised myself. I realized I was going to have to be ruthless.

"GET OUT!," I yelled.

"Make me."

I walked outside into the frigid air and I felt like my whole body was a tremor. I was amazingly strong in my course, though, no tears.

"There is not one thing you can do to change my mind. Get out of here . . . seriously, I will call the cops this time. Go, leave."

He started to cry.

"That is not going to work. Do you know how many chances I have given you? Really, I should have my fucking head examined for the shit I have put up with. I'm done . . . go . . . just leave."

I turned around, went inside, closed the door, and for the first time ever at my parents' house I actually threw the lock on it.

I bolted to the kitchen for some water and to my relief heard the truck pull away. I also heard my dad's footsteps.

"Hey, Dad."

"Can't sleep?"

"No. Derrick stopped by."

"WHAT?!"

"Dad, it's OK, really. I did it, I told him . . . " Now the tears. *"He is not going to just crawl away from me and accept this. I seriously need to get out of here early."*

"GODDAMNIT!"

"Hey, Dad, I get it, but really . . . there is nothing, not a thing, that you can do. I just have to get back to Vermont and avoid his calls. He'll get the picture eventually. I honestly feel so much better that you guys know. I can't tell you how sorry I am. I know this must be awful for you and Mom."

"Sweetie, you don't need to worry about us. We are sorry, of course, but we are proud of your strength and resolve. I'll make sure you are awake early. Leave Greenwich, you're right. If that son of a bitch as much as lifts a finger . . . "

"Dad, it's OK." We hugged and I really felt bad. I could tell this was eating at him. He must want to kill Derrick. I really didn't think about how they would respond. I mean, I am not even sure I knew I was going to tell them. I feel way better though . . . like there is no turning back now . . . it really is over.

ToDAY I CAN almost imagine the conversation they might have had that night when pillows were providing a cushion from their pain. Together they bushwhacked a clearing in their hearts for their now-fragile daughter. I wonder still if they knew that night that my escape to school was clearly not about my desire for an education. Did they predict the sleep that would follow? Did they know that I would head back to school and crawl into bed for nearly three months? My battered state of mind would render me incapable of breaking the silence that isolated me and left me trapped in an internal power struggle of shame and blame. The silence served no one, least of all me.

Upon My Devotion

Upon my devotion
you spread your anger
with the world
I now suffer

You thought you were safe
or perhaps you thought
I wouldn't stop kidding myself

Memories well up
your ice-green eyes bulging
your once-soft hands
twisting,
shoving,
pinning my body . . . my mind

Close to three years fear bound me to you
Fear of being alone, fear of losing
all I have invested in "us"

Close to three years

I was the butt
of your anger
—my instinct was first to protect you—
I believed in your promises
My belief has deteriorated
and an even greater fear
has pulled me away

Losing sight of myself
I always put you first
I leave you yes
but that is a far less sacrifice
then leaving myself
I am not capable of being
responsible for you and me both

This time . . .
I choose me
Forever

—ELIN STEBBINS

––––––

Shutting the door on my relationship was not the same as shutting my mind. Eventually my tough exterior mask fell, and behind it were these words I wrote to my parents while they were on vacation. I was finally to the point where I could admit to them that things were out of control.

Dear Mom and Dad,

I am home right now from school and have been since Wednesday. Though I hate to admit all that's happening I think I finally have to. I have been trying to be really strong and stand on my own but I know now that I am not capable.

My thoughts are really in my way and I need to turn to you two to help me. Aside from being lonely, too much has happened in my life. I really feel like I am going nuts.

I need to head back to school today, but tomorrow I am going to see if I can talk to one of the school counselors. I have been really trying to solve my problems on my own, but I just can't.

I really need help. Whether it comes from you or someone else I don't know. What I do know is I need help. At this point I am lost. Between Derrick and my former life and trying so hard to adjust to being in school, it's just all too much.

I am so sorry and I feel guilty knowing that you will go home from your trip to find this letter but I didn't know what else to do. I am also sorry that I am not strong enough to deal with this on my own. Please call me.

I love you.

Elin

Hi,

So it's set up. Mom called the school after I gave her the name of the therapist and she called to say that I have an appointment. Be careful what you wish for, you just might get it . . . or I think that is the saying? I know I need the help but now I am dreading the appointment. I still can't even believe this is me.

Hey,

I met with the counselor/shrink. She (Jane) is nice, but I have such a hard time talking about all of this. She told me to start at the beginning, and I just kind of melted in to the chair, trying to swim to that place. It's like crossing the English Channel . . . cold, huge, dark, and rough. I don't know how I will be able to really describe this to her. My God, I can hardly even describe it to myself.

"Elin, I first want to establish that you are safe in this room. In essence, what you choose to share with me here is between you and me. Your mother indicated that you were involved in a . . . turbulent . . . relationship and she is hopeful that your wanting to take an active role in therapy will help see you to a place where you feel whole."

Feel whole? What is that like? I am Swiss cheese here. Where do I begin? I have hardly left the beach and the water is already over my head.

"I am sensing some discomfort. Why don't we start there . . . describe how you feel about being here today."

Deep breath . . . I agreed to do this.

"Um . . . well . . . I suppose ashamed . . . that's how I feel. You know, like a loser. I always figured I could handle my own problems. I really never expected that I would land on this spot, you know? I mean, like I would never have thought this when I was little . . . I just was so much stronger."

"Stronger? How so?"

"I guess if you could see a picture of who I was compared to who I turned out to be, you might not think that we were the same person."

"Ah, yet you are. Since I can't see 'the picture,' how about you describe it for me?"

"Well yeah . . . I know they're both me . . . well sort of but not . . . I mean, I don't want to be this version of myself. As for the picture, it's like when I was little, I was really happy, I was full of energy and nothing felt like a super-big challenge. I actually helped my friends. But now? I feel ancient and tired and sick inside, and I am so far gone that I am in therapy. I hate this version of me."

"What version is that?"

"The one that is scared to fall asleep for fear of the dream that might *occur, the version that flinches when someone moves to brush hair away from my eyes, the version that can't think of anything but crawling into bed and not engaging with the world, the version that can't find humor in anything, the version that distrusts people. That version."*

"Let's talk a little bit about the shame. Why do you suppose you feel ashamed?"

"Because I allowed it. Derrick, well, he had a really bad temper and I didn't end it. I just stayed and I feel ashamed because now my parents know . . . and now they will know that I am not that strong person. I couldn't leave him."

"You are here today, yes?"

"Well, yeah, but it took a lot of time to get here . . . and it's hard to trust it. I mean, I have accepted his excuses before and he has managed to get me back. I think I would just die for real if I went back to him now. I mean, I won't but it's scary still."

"Why do you believe you stayed?"

"I have asked myself that question a lot lately. Somehow when I got to school, it was like I could see it all for the first time. I think somehow I was surviving. Enduring. I really don't know, but he threatened a lot of things. I guess I believed he was capable of following through on the threats . . . you know, somehow I didn't see them as idle."

"What kind of threats?"

"Oh . . . gosh . . . you name it. He'd kill me, he'd kill himself, he'd kill us both, kill the dog, he would always find a way to be near me, he'd follow me, he'd hurt my family. I guess I felt held hostage on some level. I believed him, you know?"

"I can only imagine how frightening that must have been. Tell me, are you frightened of those things still?"

"Oddly enough, not really. Since I got to school, it's almost like I could see him for what he really is . . . a scared little boy. I don't think he really has the ability to hurt himself . . . I mean, like kill himself or me. I think he will hurt himself in other ways—drugs and alcohol—but not buying a gun or eating pills."

"So you think he will escape his own pain by fogging the mirror with drugs and alcohol?"

"Yeah, sadly, I do."

"Elin, this is a great start. I hope you can feel good about your decision to embark on this journey. Many people remain in abusive relationships. The mere fact that you have taken large steps to not only terminate the relationship but also look at what led up to it is remarkable. Truly I hope you can feel good about that."

"Thanks, I am trying. So, what's next?"

"If this time works for you, then we will solidify it as a standing appointment as long as you would like to be here."

"OK, then I will see you next week?"

"You bet. Have a great week."

So onward to my great week I march. I cannot begin to describe how exhausted I am. I cannot even comprehend staying awake even another five minutes.

———

Hi,

The whole thing with Charlie is a joke. I mean, we had the library night—no big deal—and one other kind of mess-around-some-but-nothing-all-that-freakish, and now I can't even begin to understand him. He's super unapproachable and seems to want to just shut me out. He literally avoids me . . . whatever! I mean he was the one that sought me out. It was sort of flattering and all but now it's like a big f-you. Fine . . . I really am not up for that/this. Either we are friends or we aren't. What is it with the guys I get involved with? For Christ's sake, do I have "Mess with my head" written all over me or what! Maybe he can see how pathetic I am? Ugh!!!!!

I keep thinking about the meeting with Jane and what she asked me. Why do I think I stayed? I look back and I honestly don't have a clue. I was so surprised by it all. I was so scared . . . scared to stay, scared to leave. I wanted to be on my own . . . I made a huge deal about it to my parents. Now that I am here in Vermont, it's sort of surreal, like it happened but not to me almost. I just can't believe it. Really, who allows someone to hit them? Certainly not a Stebbins. I was supposed to be amazing . . . yeah, amazingly stupid. I still think about how when I first got together with Derrick he was so pissed at Mark. What a liar! I thought he was so heroic . . . some hero! I don't know. I really just don't know at all.

Hi,

Wow, what a really cool night. A few of us piled in my car and went over to this bar that everyone calls The Library. Isabel said it was so people could say you are going to the library in front of the staff and they wouldn't know what you were talking about. Anyway, it's this funky bar that is located in the basement of an old house. There's a pool table and shuffleboard. It's actually really great. We all hung out, had some fun, and then when we drove home, the coolest thing happened. The moon is full and there is snow everywhere so it is super bright outside. Of course all the roads are dirt covered in snow and there is no traffic anywhere. Doug dares me to turn off the headlights, so I do, and we drove down the road but could see almost like it was day. I only did it for a little bit but it was scary fun . . . kind of exhilarating. When we got back to campus we had a huge snowball fight. It's the most fun I have had in a long time. For a second I actually felt normal, like I was just a kid away at school with friends.

But then I get back to my room and there's a note on my bed saying, "Derrick called." I wish he would just flippin' leave me alone!

It's a "red-light day." I know it from the moment I wake at an ungodly 4:30 a.m. It sets me off, groping back to bed from the bathroom. I scold Chinook. "It is not even close to breakfast time. Go back to bed!" I hiss with a snap that says "Get out!" I see her dark shadow bolt from me as if

I have shocked her. Under the covers again, I sigh. There is no going back to sleep. Alright! Get up.

Downstairs I flip on the lights, coffeemaker, computer. My mood is improving, and sensing that, Chinook looks eagerly toward her bowl. "No, you are not eating at this hour. You will be starving by dinner time." She slinks to her downstairs bed. She stares at me from her blanket and I can almost hear her say, "Life's not fair. How come you get coffee and I get squat?" Tough! You are a dog.

There. That feels better and clears it all up, I am sure, for her.

Time passes and Kodiak joins me. We have our breakfast routine down and enjoy our ritual of sharing the start of the day.

Now it's Chandler's turn. She's been sick, nothing awful, just a bug. The thermometer confirms there is no fever. I see her shaking off her own red-light mood that beckons for her to stay home another day. And she is gone . . . off to school.

Jimmy's absorbed in his work and Chinook and I head out for our run. When we reach the light that I already saw in my mind, we wait for what feels like an eternity: pause, think, what am I missing? I unconsciously push the start button on my watch and time begins again. We barrel across the street and take the trail that prevents a major hill climb. All the birds are out and I marvel at their energy. So glad we made it out here today.

Laziness safely behind me, I think about how I really almost "missed" Jimmy, how in that first blush I couldn't see *him*. Or was it me I couldn't see?

It's 1993, during an early-November snowfall in the valley of Vail, Colorado. I am struggling to control many internal voices: *Just do it. People go to bars alone all the time. I've been to the Red Lion a zillion times, with friends, with Hunter, but never alone . . . I can do this! NO. I am scared. What if someone talks to me? What if no one talks to me? For God's sake,* shut up . . . *just go in!*

Of course the doorman doesn't card me. *I must really look thirty now. OK, I can do this. Man, is it ever packed in here. Walk up to the bar, Stebbins, and order a frickin' beer!*

"What'll you have?"

*Shoot, is Mr. Bartender talking to me or the guy next to me? Oh, it's me.
He has a nice smile.*

"Umm, do you guys have micro beer?"

"Wha wha wha wha wha."

*Oh my God, what the hell did he just say? Who talks that fast? Shoot, he's
waiting for me to answer.*

"I'm sorry, what?"

"You wanna taste it?"

"Sure, OK, yeah . . . " *He is not listening to me; in fact he just walked
away. I have already failed at the alone-in-a-bar thing. Wait, here he comes.
Oh, he's handing me a taste . . .*

"Thanks!" *I guess this is good. Now what?*

"I'm sorry, what?"

"You want one?"

"Sure . . . "

"Twelve ounces or twenty-three?" *Mr. Interrogation. How many questions do I have to answer?*

"Um . . . twelve?"

Gone again . . . back again . . . and I pay.

*Where the hell am I going to sit . . . oh, there's a stool at the bar . . . I guess
I can do this.*

Jimmy, aka Mr. Bartender, later told me that he watched me walk to
the stool and he knew. In that moment he saw "me."

"Excuse me . . . is this stool taken?" The guy next to it shakes his head.
I grab the stool. *I am sitting at a bar alone, and I do not know anyone. Why
was this a great idea?*

The bar is packed and there is a never-ending stream of people funnel-
ing in, all of whom seem to know "Mr. Bartender." "Jimmy!" they hail
him as they enter. After a while, I can't help commenting to my barstool
neighbor, whom by now I have come to know by name.

"So, Danny, who is this guy, the mayor or something?"

"Who, Jimmy?"

"Yeah, *Jimmy*, the bartender, the blond. Every person who walks
through the door calls out, 'JIMMY!' like he's a long-lost friend or something."

"That's Jimmy Waldal. He's awesome, super friendly. Everyone in town knows him. Really great guy, ya know?"

"Ah, bartender. Yeah, I guess everyone would want to know him, huh?"

"He's not just a bartender. He also owns a mountain bike shop here in the Valley." I am really watching him now. *Mountain bike shop owner? Hmmm, so not a lost soul type? Oh shit! He just totally busted me!!! I swear to God, what an idiot I am!* I am staring at this Jimmy guy's butt and I slowly look up and he is staring at me staring at his butt . . . in the mirror! Now we are smiling, and he's pointing at me in the mirror, like *I caught you.*

That was the beginning of what Jimmy describes as his uphill battle to win my heart.

A couple of weeks later I had left my six-year-old home alone after he cried that he just did *not* want to go to the store to buy milk. First, I made him swear to not answer the phone or the door. He swore and I left, drove like a bat out of hell, bought the flippin' milk, and drove home like a bat out of hell. I walked through the door and my sweet boy handed me a note that he'd written in crayon—Jimmy and all the numbers that would ring Jimmy's house. After I blasted Max for answering the phone—not once, I learned, but three times—I held that little note and imagined the whole thing. First the greeting, "No, my mommy's not here," agreeing to take a message, dropping the receiver, probably on the vinyl floor of our kitchen, scrambling of feet, hunting for the crayon, hunting for the paper, and then the writing. I can still see him writing with his tongue just barely revealed between lips pursed in concentration . . . one number at a time. Hmm, Jimmy had to be patient. The other two male callers just said they'd call back.

I returned Jimmy's call and agreed to our first date. It was one of those dinners where the conversaton is effortless and in what felt like minutes we realized we were the only customers left in the restaurant.

Our second date became what we now lovingly refer to as "The Stool Conversation," another flagrant attempt on my part to "miss" Jimmy. After going to a party together, we arrived back at my condo, lit a fire, opened some wine, put on music . . . and Jimmy, of course, had visions of some wonderful romantic evening. That scratching noise a record needle makes when dragged across an LP—I suppose that is what he heard when I ducked an attempt at our first kiss, grabbed a little fireplace stool, sat on it, and began to explain how I just wanted to be friends.

"You know, I am leaving soon, I think I told you. I'm going to be gone for a while—maybe even six months. I just don't see how I have room for a boyfriend." He is just sitting there staring at me, not saying anything.

OK, hurting people *sucks*.

"Are you going to say anything?" *Please don't be mad at me . . .*

"There's really nothing to say. It's cool . . . friends. I see it differently but I am not about begging or changing your mind."

Pretty much we went to bed, he on the couch and me in my room. As I stared at the ceiling I filtered the evening through my head. Jimmy's image weighed on my mind . . . all the "red lights" I had flashed for him with my hand and now the talk by the fireplace. *Shit! He is way too nice for me . . .*

OK, Elin, what did you just say? Too nice? Are you flippin' kidding me? Like what the hell is too nice? With those thoughts marching through my head, I eventually fell asleep.

Night gave way to morning, and in the early light I think I actually *saw* him for the first time, if only briefly. I could feel it, like the flutter of an eyelash: What if?

From there, Jimmy didn't give up. He wrote me a letter that outlined his need to put into perspective friendship versus the "crush" he had on me. He called me, I called him, and when we talked minutes turned to hours and every time we hung up my hand stretched just a little further toward him. It was like kids on a beach digging a tunnel toward each other. You dig and dig until there's a little hole and the tip of your friend's finger touches the tip of yours and you continue digging until you clasp hands.

With unwavering patience and care, Jimmy removed the blocks of the wall I had built around my wounded heart. It took another month or so, but in time the notion that "nice" was somehow a character flaw dissolved into the cold Colorado air.

Hi,

Sitting outside her closed office door makes my heart race. "I am in therapy!" Oh my God, like who needs therapy? There is a soft chorus of voices behind the door, almost like a whisper. Who else does she see? Whoever walks out, they will know that I need therapy. Ah, but conversely I, too, will know that they need it. Hmm.

"Elin?"

Blink, and there's Jane looking hopeful and annoyingly proud of me or something. I see a figure's back edging out the door, and it occurs to me that I missed it. This other therapy-needing type saw me with my eyes closed and all I got was a glimpse of their vanishing back.

"Elin?"

"Hey, Jane. Sorry, I was lost in thought, I guess. How are you?" Good, get up, smile, you are your mother's daughter. Be polite!

"No apology necessary. Come on in, make yourself comfortable."

It's like she just doesn't get the fact that there could be a roaring fireplace and down bed complete with a down comforter sitting in here and I would not be comfortable.

"How was your week?"

So we are jumping back into this. How was my week? I guess I'll skip the moonlit drive. She may think I am suicidal and willing to take friends with me.

"I guess you could say OK."

"OK. Now what would you say?"

Oh my God, do they learn this crap in therapy school?

"What I would say? Well, Jane, I think I would say average."

"Help me see what that's like for you."

OK, how to find the 3-D glasses for her to "see" my average week.

"Jane, bear with me here. I am so not used to this. I mean, I run around with all my jumbled thoughts, like in-a-blender jumbled, and getting you to 'see' my average—that's tough."

"I can wait."

Well of course she can. She's getting paid to listen to my miserable thoughts. I, on the other hand, am suffering over here. What to say to make her see?

"Well, there's a guy in one of my classes and he . . . he seems to judge me. You know, like somehow what I write about, he doesn't believe me or something. It really bothers me. I mean, he should be focused on his own stuff but he's written now three poems and they are all a series of quips about this wretched girl who is whining about how hateful her boyfriend was but really she is a silver-spoon-fed brat from a hoity town who hasn't a clue." There, that is it. I want to hurt that guy.

"And you know that these 'quips,' as you say, are about you?"

"No, I mean he hasn't told me, but he always seems to look at me when he finishes reading aloud, and I just sense a judgment. Somehow my pain has provided him his own version of inspiration, but it's so mean. I really think he is awful. I just . . . well I haven't gone to class all week now. I don't want his wandering-eyed judgment."

"Let's just say for argument's sake that you're mistaken—he is actually writing about his own girlfriend who has rejected him. But you feel like a safe harbor to land on when he finishes because you, too, have taken a risk to share what is painful and somehow liberated him. So really his eyes landing on you bring him comfort. How does that feel?"

"Nice try."

"I'm not just trying here, Elin. I want you to picture it, the same way you allowed me to envision you in that classroom."

"Jane, I can't stand this guy. I mean, I have nicknamed him Ezra Pound behind his back. He is pompous. There is no way I am safe harbor. I honestly can't picture it."

"Try—see the other side."

I need to close my eyes for this. I am seriously rewinding the cassette tape in my brain trying to "see it," will myself to "see it." There's Ezra . . . he's reading . . . all at once I look at the page he is holding and I can see that it is shaking . . . he is trembling . . . now I look at his eyes and they are cast down *on the page . . . he is over-annunciating, for effect, I think . . . and he looks first at the professor . . . and then at me . . . and now his eyes light again on the page. Am I so self-absorbed that I missed something? Deep breath . . .*

"Alright, I see it. Perhaps there is a different perspective out there."

"What did you see?"

"I noticed his hand trembling while he was reading, you know, like somehow he is scared or heartbroken but pissed off or, who knows, just writing for writing's sake. Maybe it's really not about me. Oh yeah, no one else in the room is looking at him. They are all examining their own papers and I am the only one listening—listening with my eyes anyway."

She's smiling at me now, like somehow she witnessed me crawling. No, not quite crawling. I am the little baby on the floor with its mouth wrapped around the shag carpet fibers . . . not quite crawling. I babysat for a baby like that, you know, he was in that stuck phase? The arms and legs are all moving but the stomach is glued to the floor and he would use his mouth to somehow navigate what he was experiencing. I can see him, little fists full of rug, and it occurs to me that I have everything in common with him, that little baby from my babysitting days.

I CAN PICTURE Jimmy standing in the kitchen, work gloves on, clothes dirtied from yard work. "Do you want to see a hummingbird nest?"

"Sure, let me grab the camera." We retreat to the backyard and he pushes the fronds of a robelini palm to reveal his discovery. Ohhhhh, I see it, it's tiny. I look around to see if the mother is buzzing nearby, but no, she is not.

"Look how little it is. Wow . . . "

"Yeah, they popped their little heads up and I could see them." I take a step onto the wall to get a better view and Jimmy helps me negotiate an opening for the lens. I know it immediately; I have the wrong lens. I need a macro lens, the kind that allows these miniscule treasures to be captured, what ordinary people would miss were it not for a photographer.

"Shoot, I am too close for this lens."

"Can you see how many babies there are?"

"No, it's really hard to tell. Wow, hard to believe they really are *in* there." I marvel at the knowledge that life is nestled in this nest that is the size of a giant's thimble. I take a picture anyway. Evidence? Pictures frame our experiences yet they really don't. The picture is missing so many other elements, like the gentle way Jimmy holds back the fronds, or the earthy smell tickling my nose, the way my ears are waiting to hear the buzz of a worried mother hummingbird. I step from the wall, leaving them in peace.

"Pretty cool . . . ," he says, almost as if it were a question.

"Yeah, really cool. Thanks."

"You bet."

Back in the house I turn to watch as he bends over to retrieve more yard clippings. He looks so at peace, somehow in his element, and I am pierced by his grace and enthusiasm over the wonders that exist.

Hi,

School's over—doesn't look as if I will be going back. Especially since John hired me to work for him at the new bank. Suzy is there so it has been easy to step right back into the routine. Kind of funny how some of our old customers are opening up accounts over here—I am sure John helped with that but Suzy and I like to think they like seeing us, too.

My new apartment is just up the street from Meadow Wood, kind of ironic really.

I just wasn't up for school. I mean I am glad I went—really it probably saved my life—just getting the hell out of here.

I told Suzy all about Derrick and she mentioned she remembers asking me about bruises on my arm and how I pulled my sleeve down and told her I had fallen and she believed me. Now that she knows—she wonders why she believed me. She said she just never would have thought that would happen to me. It felt good to tell her, she did say it explained a lot, you know how he was always lurking outside the bank, and how I would never go out without him for a girl's night. It's nice to have a friend just accept it—you know, not judge me.

Anyway—back in Greenwich again.

THE IMPORTANCE OF ritual is never clearer than when it is challenged. The other night while Max was home from school a debate ensued that left Kodiak and me feeling a bit defensive. The subject was whether I should be making breakfast for Kodiak, who is in the eighth grade.

Max's position vaguely reminded me of things my own siblings may have said: "When I was your age . . . " followed by a list of items they were either subjected to or deprived of. Max made it sound as if he was bor-der-line neglected when he was Kodiak's age. He maintained I am cod-dling his brother, a habit he is certain will set Kodiak up for failure when he heads to college. The situation was only made worse by Jimmy and Chandler, who decided Max was right. In the end it was Kodiak who got the short end of the stick. He ultimately left the room feeling completely misunderstood and, with a burst of anger, went to bed. Later I sat with him and we each agreed that regardless of who cooks breakfast, not only was our time together important to each of us, it was non-negotiable.

I have had time to reflect now and what keeps coming back to me is the conversation that Kodiak and I had days before the argument during our sacred thirty-minute ritual called breakfast.

His study of Martin Luther King Jr. and my thinking about how boys view manhood were the main ingredients of the conversation that unfolded. Kodiak had to write a speech for English, something along the lines of MLK's "I Have a Dream" speech. And I wanted to know what he thought about what it meant to be a man, so I asked him.

He was quiet, so quiet that it actually crossed my mind that he had missed the question altogether. I watched him as he finished his juice and put the glass down. He looked me square in the eyes and said, "I think it means that you have to be emotionally and intellectually really strong." I watched him as he gathered his thoughts like kindling. "I think it means playtime is over—I mean you can still have fun, but it's time to think about what and how you are going to contribute to the world."

Wow. My heart was racing and I was holding my breath for fear that I could blow this incredible moment.

"I also think that a man would put his own life in the way of danger to keep his family safe." He was quiet. I could tell he was still thinking but he was looking at me as if he wanted to know what I thought.

"Kodiak, I really like what you said, how you feel. Let me ask you one more question: what about love? Do you think a man needs to be loving and nurturing?"

"Absolutely. I feel so lucky because Dad is so loving and supportive. I definitely think a man needs to be loving and nurturing."

"I think you just found the topic for your speech, Kodiak. What do you think?"

"Yeah! That's a great idea, I need to think about that some but you may be right."

With that he was off to brush his teeth and scramble off to the bus. I sat in that spot for a while thinking about him, what a remarkable person he is.

We can raise boys with a different perspective. One mind at time, we can help boys really feel comfortable in their own skins and understand fully that being a man isn't about being macho. Then maybe, little by little, our world will change for the better.

The rest of the family is right about one thing. At nearly fourteen, Kodiak can make his own breakfast. But I wouldn't trade our time for anything.

Hi,

I'm running. At first it feels like it is as fast as I can go but I can hear him . . .

"Stop! Elin, stop! I swear to God if you don't stop I will hunt you down and kill you."

My feet feel as if they are five thousand pounds each. I am slowing to the point where I can hear his footfalls behind me. I can feel my shoulders brace for the blow, and I open my mouth to scream but nothing comes out.

My eyes open and it is dark. I am breathing heavily and I am covered in sweat. The covers are all wound around my legs and I lift myself up on one elbow to rip myself from the bedding. Flopping back down on my back I glance at the clock. It's 2:36 a.m.

"I'm safe," I say out loud to the empty room. With legs that feel ancient, I rise and navigate toward the kitchen and flip on the light. The apartment is still. After pouring a glass of water, I stoop to splash my face.

"I'm awake," I say, again to no one.

This recurring dream—well, nightmare—not so sure why I have to be tormented when my eyes are closed. It's almost always the same. Derrick is chasing me. I am afraid. My feet are heavy and running is hard. I have no voice. I am trying to scream but nothing escapes. I can feel him gaining on me. Just before he delivers a blow, I wake up.

No doubt it was the TV show, earlier today. I saw a program, one of those talk shows, and they were talking about women who stay with men who hit them. There were people in the audience who maintained they would never stay with a guy who hit them. I felt as if I could have been any one of those people . . . that girl from long ago that I was. Confidence that was like a badge, you know, something I could just whip out and it said it all: "I am strong! So strong I have this shiny emblem of strength to prove it."

What people don't seem to get is the guy doesn't haul off and hit you on your first date. First there is the falling in love, followed by the extreme need, and then there's this slow erosion of self until without noticing it, the woman becomes unrecognizable even to herself.

I have heard stories about people who have had a limb amputated. They will tell you that they still feel the limb. It itches, it aches, it twitches . . . but it's not there. That's what losing myself was like. I could feel it but I had no access to it. I never felt more alone in all my life than during my relationship with Derrick.

The most symbolic part of the dream is that I have no voice. I had no voice back then. All my tears were shed alone. I was so afraid to tell anyone—what if he followed through on his threats? Also if I told anyone then I would not be who they thought I was . . . strong. And I could not love him into being a different person. One raised by a loving family free from pain and violence. In the end I was powerless to change him. You know, when I met him I felt like I knew him. I was so drawn to him initially. There was the party where he saved me from Mark . . . As if it were yesterday I can feel how special he made me feel in that moment, like someone who was worthy of rescue.

It's ironic really that that auspicious start led to my own need to save myself. Maybe I was slow, maybe I was scared, maybe I had no voice, but I did it. I saved myself. I found my voice. I found my legs. And with my own strength, I started over, without him.

Maybe the dream is a reminder that we all walk through storms? I saved myself . . . I am my own hero. And you know . . . I forgive myself. I forgive myself for not choosing the underground shelter of the storm cellar, and really, I am so proud of myself for hanging on while the tornado tore apart everything I knew. Against all odds, with everything I had, once the quiet returned, I got back up with dirt, blood, and skin under my nails, by dragging one leg at a time onto the ground that would be a new foundation to stand on. Devastation around me, but body intact . . . I picked up the pieces and now here I am assembling my life with a heart full of promise.

When I think of people who survive the devastation of a tornado, what comes to mind is their resolve to begin again. They look to either side of them and clasp hands with their loved ones and ask for help. As a community they pick up the rubble, they rebuild, they begin again.

Looking outside my window I can see that dawn is spreading across the sky. I have a voice, I will heal, I have help, and I will help others.

MIDNIGHT STRETCHES LIKE a blanket over our home. I have awakened from a dream that still feels within my grasp, and I lay motionless in an effort to pull it back to me. It remains beyond reach, however, much like a ball that has rolled under a couch that outstretched fingers only push farther into the abyss. I flop onto my back knowing that along with the dream, sleep will elude me. The rain outside our bedroom window blends with each breath that Jimmy takes, providing a lullaby of life, a chorus accompanying my roaming thoughts.

I shift to my side and stare at him. Despite the dark that envelops us I can see his profile. His features are so familiar I could trace them by memory even now in the dark: smiling eyes, perfect teeth, chiseled chin, blondish grey hair.

Having lost the battle to hold onto my own dream, I imagine his. He could be a whole myriad of places: at the beach playing catch with our kids, fishing off the coast with friends, working, or perhaps he is at our cabin. Yes that's it. I go to him, and invite him to join me on the dock.

There the dream remains, with us basking in the glory of a sunset and the utter joy we share in each other's company.

Right after Derrick, I could not imagine that I would ever find a man who would be all I desire: my best friend, lover, soul mate, strong, nurturing, confident, and completely steadfast in his love for me and our life together. Together we have built a home where love, safety and loyalty are the foundation. Watching him I feel as if I am the luckiest woman alive, and my gratitude for him is without measure.

The rain picks up and I burrow into Jimmy's warmth. Without waking he wraps his arm over my waist and tucks me into the peace that is our marriage.

By the time I was able to truly extricate myself from my relationship with Derrick I was nearly twenty. Ending it invoked both courage and fear in almost equal measure. A series of steps led to my true emancipation, steps that had he been a hair more violent could have cost me my life. In those days information was scarce and I certainly did not employ a safety plan to end the relationship. I had never heard of "dating abuse." Like the rest of the world I was in denial; things like that just didn't happen to a girl like me, a girl raised by loving people in a community better known for Ivy League educations than for cuts and bruises. Denial was the mask I wore to survive a beating and still love myself. But as with all masks, there was a place—even if but a pinprick in diameter—to see through to where the truth lay. The truth was that I—not someone else's daughter, sister, friend but I—was a victim of abuse.

The depression that settled on me over the epiphany that I was a statistic, a formerly battered woman, was painful. It slowed everything in my life almost to a standstill. Charlie at school told me that my entire body slumped. He listed his observations almost cruelly: you drag your feet to the point of scuffing, your shoulders are hunched, you cover your mouth when you are talking as if you are embarrassed to be heard, everything about you tells the world that there is self-loathing behind those beautiful green eyes. Ouch. I got help, first from the counselor at school, then from a therapist in Greenwich after I left school. During my separation from Hunter, I saw a therapist in Boulder who for two years helped me with the dismantling of my first marriage. Altogether five years of much-needed therapy, which put me on a path to forgive myself and realize that my attempts to own responsibility for what had taken place were simply another form of victim blaming. It had happened, and like all things it was a part of me—but it did not have to define me.

There was a period when I was very angry. I resented the years that Derrick stole from me. I was angry that he could walk around and enjoy the freedom to begin a new relationship and repeat his violence. I hated him for a while, too. He was the reason my marriage was failing, he was the reason I trembled when someone as much as raised their voice, he was the reason for all of my insecurities. That didn't work, though; the more I ran around on the crutches of blame and anger, the worse I felt. I had to get past hating him and blaming him. It simply sucked too much energy from me.

I wanted to shout to the world that domestic violence runs rampant in every corner of every town. When I was in my early twenties I provided community outreach to a women's shelter. I now can see that in large part I had made a deal with myself: if I can help people, then I can go back to the way I was before all of this affected me. No such luck; internal negotiations that have a contingency are doomed. I had to end any form of self-imposed bargaining and absorb into my being that despite the cruelty I was free to live my life—not as damaged goods—but as a whole woman rich with countless experiences. The liberation that followed years later was really the light at the proverbial end of the tunnel. True acceptance is what pulled me forward and gave birth to my voice. I am a woman whose life was shaped by many things, one of which is an abusive relationship. Its full impact on me cannot be plucked with tweezers like a splinter from a finger. Instead it is just a piece of the puzzle that has created this beautiful, if sometimes messy, life. I did not get to this crossroads alone; I have my parents, siblings, friends, children, and husband to thank for their unwavering belief in me, and I remain humbled and eternally grateful.

POSTSCRIPT

WE ARE AT our cabin on Whidbey Island and it is December. The pads of my bare feet remind me that outdoors the temperature hovers in the low thirties. Socks, sweater, blanket, and a window seat in the dark. It is utterly still. The large kitchen window that faces west is divided. The small panes of glass provide sixteen different vignettes. Supported by the pillows of the window seat, I place my chin on the sill. A single pine tree lines up with the moon, shading me from the near-halogen brilliance it casts off. Yet if I sit straight up and choose the next pane I am near squinting for the beam is squarely in my sight.

I feel somehow exposed in the spotlight. I pinch myself—there is no other me anywhere. My experiences have all led to this single epiphany and I embrace the path I have walked. The lines I have skipped over, the truths I have raked up, the "me" I have become. Out of the turmoil of abuse came strength, and I have the gift to share that potency.

Along with my husband, family, and friends, my own children are completely aware of the serpentine route I have traveled and they love me exactly as I am, as do I. Had I not had the courage to forgive myself for my perceived weaknesses, I am not sure the taste of strength would be so pure. In some ways its purity comes from being a mother, the impenetrable need to make the world a safer place for my children. I am a richer person for the "all of it" and that knowledge rests between the beats of my heart.

The tide is high and the water is glassy, save for a ripple that shimmers in the moonlight stretching from our beach below to clear across the breadth of the harbor. I am burning with fatigue but I cannot for the life of me tear myself away from what I see. Unblinking I stare out, the twinkling light dances its magical path before me without the benefit of a breeze. The moon dips lower into the midnight sky and a shape materializes on the water.

Every hair on my body stands up as I absorb the well-lit silhouette of a tornado winking in the night. The wide top of the cone clear across the way thins as it makes its way east toward me. Pressing on the glass, my finger touches the funnel. There dancing on water is the tornado of my past bathed in moonlight. I think I was nudged awake by the silenced girl of my youth, and if I hold very still I can hear her voice reverberate across the water. In a tune as pure as a first snowfall I hear her sing to me that she is safe in the basin of a harbor. She is no longer silent.

I am not silent.

I am home, I have my voice.

ACKNOWLEDGMENTS

Writing the first draft of my memoir was equivalent to throwing up part of my life on paper; were it not for a team of individuals who actually understand readers, I fear my story would have remained unbound musings, unshared and unread. I am thankful for the many sets of eyes and minds that helped make *Tornado Warning* a reality but in a way also left an imprint on my life.

I cannot imagine this journey without the vigilance of book shepherd and BookStudio owner, Karla Olson. Wow, where do I begin, Karla? I suppose with a quote straight from an email you sent that has remained tacked to the space above my computer since the day I received it, September 18, 2009: "I have to be honest, Elin, and tell you that I am a bit mad at you right now. I stayed up about half the night reading your book . . . " You go on to tell me all the reasons you feel *Tornado Warning* will be a great book, continue with what it needs, and close by saying you would like to work with me. The single best decision I have ever made professionally is hiring you. Thank you for your friendship, belief, taking a chance, and for putting the "A" team together to bring my story to the world.

Terry Spohn, editor extraordinaire: Your drive and insistence that I come out from behind the metaphors at times nearly drove me mad, but . . . you are brilliant. Thank you for pushing me to reveal the unvarnished truths that are my beautiful (albeit somewhat messy) life. Laurie Gibson, thank you for your work and voice; you truly made me realize that my story may inspire people to take action. Claudine Mansour, words can hardly describe your vision for the cover/interior design for *Tornado Warning*; the imagery captures it. Luke Pilon and the entire Mobiah team, thank you for putting me on the Internet map! Your patience, perseverance, and creativity are appreciated and often bragged about! Thank you all . . .

There are myriad discoveries that I have made over the nearly three decades since I left the relationship I present in this book, and I am beyond appreciative for the love and support that so many have gifted me. A list of a lifetime includes many people and animals, I am both grateful and humbled to have an abundance in both categories that have helped me arrive at a place where my voice is strong enough to sing out.

My husband Jimmy and I together have built a life where mutual respect, trust, and safety are absolutes. J, were it not for your steadfast belief in my ability to turn my "pages in a box" into a story worth sharing, I fear Tornado Warning would have remained untold. It goes without saying but I will say it anyway, I love you in all my lifetimes. Thank you for your unwavering love, support, and ability to cherish all that you hold dear.

Each of my children afforded me hours of contemplation beyond counting, and relief from what sometimes felt like a rain storm without end. I love and thank you, Max, Kodiak, and Chandler. You are each lifelines of inspiration and unending joy.

Chinook, our chocolate lab (my quite unsuspecting alter ego), thank you for your willingness to run, walk, and sit with me. And to "Abby," a dog who will forever be thought of as a life ring when I needed it most.

To what I will refer to as my "readership" in the infancy of this undertaking—a private URL with posted blogs and a place to comment open to my inner-circle—your comments helped to cheer me on and push me to dig deeper when I felt like running away from ghosts. My brother Rod, your comments were spot on, immediate, and wise beyond reckoning; your place in this journey has been paramount. My sister Lorna, whose self-proclaimed "subterranean prose" also struck chords, and your unshaken belief that *Tornado Warning* was more than a personal journey but a book, was akin to having received an acceptance letter from a publisher. Additionally your countless hours of patient editorial expertise is appreciated beyond measure. Alex Furmark, I hardly remember a time when you were not with me in spirit, your support, love, cheering comments, and phone calls are all appreciated. Karen Edwards . . . oh my goodness . . . where would Tornado Warning be had you liked my first "chapter" when I thought the answer was a novel? The circular file I am certain. Thanks for the honesty, conversations, the quiet, and belief. Jeanne Bassett, you sat on our Whidbey Island porch and read cover to cover a draft that was written while you were in South America; your response and faith ushered me yet again to another level—and BTW,

I do tell you the good/bad/ugly . . . now. Suzy Dudley, my friend and co-worker during the mayhem, you kept me laughing, which helped me feel grounded, and you were one of my fiercest defenders once you knew the truth and in many ways still are. My brother Paul, thank you for being the "Rock" of support that you always are; reading the draft, the text message that followed . . . and for the coil of rope that still hinges us. My brother John, the countless telephone conversations, walks, and for the things you just "get" because . . . well, you know, just because of where we are in the constellation. Mom, you also read my draft on Whidbey Island cover to cover and in your own stalwart way bolstered me up to finish this book. As you said, "It is way too close to the bone for me to work on," and with that you encouraged me to search for an editor. Thank you for the lifetime of love and support. Dad, I only wish you were alive to share this. I can picture you, hand clenched and a loud "You tell 'em, Elin!" on your breath. I miss you so much, and thank you for your big-band-style support that reverberates still.

And a few others . . . past and present: Dee Stebbins, Ben Alexander, Kathy Warren, Nicki Waldal, Gretchen and Sony Furmark, Jim Cox, Colleen Brown, Anne Marie Stevenson, Lily Flood, Clarita Thoms-May, Hollis Peterson, Marissa Presley, Tom and Stephanie Bowman, Brooke Boardman, Bob Langan, Liz Settel, Chuck Harless, Pete and Liz Hutchinson, Shelly Clark, Boo Stearns, Jane Carlin, Tom Yahn, Margaret Meany, Christina Berger, James Israel, David Kern, Gary Shuetze, Cindy Brody, LCSW, Dr. Michael Freedman, Jess Weiner, Nancy Gruver, Amy Jussel, Kate Whitfield, Melissa Wardy, Brie Widaman, and Loren Slocum.

ABOUT THE AUTHOR

Elin Stebbins Waldal is a writer, speaker, and founder and of **girls kNOw more,** an organization whose mission is to help build confidence in middle-school-age girls.

Elin is the Love Is Not Abuse Coalition State Action Leader for California, which advocates for legislation that will require teen dating abuse curriculum in all middle schools, high schools, and colleges. She is a frequent guest on the WomenontheVerge.com radio show. She is also a regular presenter for Laura's House, an Orange County resource for victims of domestic violence. She was recognized with an Honorable Mention Award in the World of Difference Category by The San Diego County Office of Education for speaking and educating high school students. Additionally, she is a California-state-certified domestic violence advocate.

She has contributed to The Courage Network, Safe World for Women, and The Women on the Verge on-line periodicals and also serves as a *San Diego Examiner* reporter on the subject of teen dating violence.

Elin lives in Southern California with her husband, three children, and their family dog.

Reading Guide, resources, and a call to action may be found at:
www.tornadowarningbook.com